# The Canadian Living

# LIGHT
## *and*
# HEALTHY
## COOKBOOK

BY MARGARET FRASER AND THE FOOD WRITERS OF CANADIAN LIVING MAGAZINE

A CANADIAN LIVING / MADISON PRESS BOOK

Telemedia Publishing Inc.
50 Holly Street
Toronto, Ontario
Canada
M4S 3B3

**Canadian Cataloguing in Publication Data**

Fraser, Margaret
The Canadian living light and healthy cookbook

Includes index.
ISBN 0-394-22211-3

1.Cookery.  2.Nutrition.  I.Title.

RM219.F72 1991      641.5′63      C91-093075-9

Canadian Living is a trademark of Telemedia Publishing Inc.
All trademark rights, registered and unregistered, are reserved.

*On our cover: Glazed Chicken Breasts (p.64)*

**Produced by**
**Madison Press Books**
**40 Madison Avenue**
**Toronto, Ontario**
**Canada**
**M5R 2S1**

*Printed in Canada*

# Contents

# Introduction

**T**oday's cooks know how important it is to eat balanced, nutritious meals — and keep a watchful eye on fat, cholesterol and calories. But at the same time, we also want to prepare meals that look good and taste great. Now *Canadian Living* shows you just how simple and delicious healthy cooking can be. Whether you're planning a quick weekday family supper or a sophisticated dinner party, you can be sure that every dish in this easy-to-use cookbook tastes good — and is good *for* you!

Each delicious recipe featured here starts with wholesome ingredients and quick-cooking methods that preserve freshness and nutrients. Handy nutrient charts throughout help you keep track of the calories, sodium, fat and cholesterol in each serving of every recipe. And informative sidebars highlight health tips and cooking hints. We've also included a number of microwave recipes and shortcuts. Whether it's a lighter, healthier version of a family favorite or new dishes created especially for this book, each recipe has been carefully tested so you can be sure of good results every time.

One of the most important goals for good health is to reduce the total amount of fat you consume in a day. And that's not as hard as it sounds, when you follow the guidelines our food writers and test kitchen staff used in compiling the recipes for this book:

**1.** Wherever possible, reduce the amount of fat used as an ingredient and in cooking methods.
**2.** When a little fat is required, choose cooking oils such as canola, safflower, sunflower, corn and olive oil.
**3.** Use dairy products that are lower in fat. Buy milk, yogurt and cottage cheese with a butterfat (B.F.) or milk fat (M.F.) content of 2% or less, light sour cream and cream cheese, and cheeses with a butterfat (B.F.) content of less than 15%.
**4.** Buy lean cuts of meat and remove all visible fat before cooking. Use cooking methods that preserve nutrients and require little or no fat: steam, poach, grill, roast, bake or stir-fry.
**5.** Make sure your meals include lots of high-fiber (low in fat) grains, legumes, fruits and vegetables.

Eating light, however, is more than just cutting back on fat and calories. It's also a matter of eating right — so we've included menu suggestions that make it easy for you to put together nutritious meals with fresh, good-for-you ingredients. And the handy nutrient chart with every recipe also shows you the protein, calcium, fiber and iron in each serving.

Eating lighter and healthier is part of the lifestyle of the '90s. We hope the appealing recipes and the food and health tips we've featured in this cookbook will make it easy for you to enjoy good food — *and* good health!

**Margaret Fraser**

# High-Energy Breakfasts

**G**et yourself — and your day — off to a high-energy start by taking the time to have a good breakfast. Whether it's a cool and quick Fruit and Yogurt Shake on the run or a sit-down bowl of Jiffy Muesli with milk and fresh fruit, each deliciously light, easy-to-make recipe in this section provides the nutrition your body needs. That's why breakfast is still the most important meal of the day — it's food to *go* on!

## Big Batch Bran Muffins

**Per Muffin:**

Calories: 241

Fat: 7.3 g

Protein: 4.9 g

Carbohydrate: 43.3 g

Calcium: 61 mg

Iron: 2.9 mg

Fiber: 4.4 g

Sodium: 450 mg

Cholesterol: 25 mg

*Keep a quantity of batter in the refrigerator so you can make fresh, hot muffins for breakfast, lunch or snacks. This recipe comes from the Maritimes and has a pleasant molasses tang.*

| 3 cups | natural bran | 750 mL |
|---|---|---|
| 3 cups | all-bran cereal | 750 mL |
| 2 cups | boiling water | 500 mL |
| 3 cups | buttermilk | 750 mL |
| 1-1/2 cups | granulated sugar | 375 mL |
| 1 cup | vegetable oil | 250 mL |
| 1 cup | fancy molasses | 250 mL |
| 4 | eggs, beaten | 4 |
| 5 cups | all-purpose flour | 1.25 L |
| 5 tsp | baking soda | 25 mL |
| 1 tbsp | salt | 15 mL |
| 2 cups | raisins or chopped dates | 500 mL |

■ In large bowl, combine natural bran and bran cereal. Stir in boiling water to moisten; let cool for 10 minutes. Stir in buttermilk, sugar, oil, molasses and eggs.

■ In separate large bowl, combine flour, baking soda and salt; mix in raisins. Add to bran mixture, stirring until evenly mixed. Cover tightly and refrigerate for up to 1 week.

■ To make muffins, spoon batter into large greased or paper-lined muffin cups, filling to top. Bake in 375°F (190°C) oven for about 25 minutes or until firm to the touch. Makes 36 muffins.

---

**YUMMY YOGURT**

If you're an adult over 35, you need milk as much as teens and children do. The lactose and vitamin D found in milk aid in absorbing the calcium that's needed to maintain healthy bones.

But if you don't like milk, try low-fat yogurt instead. It's an excellent source of calcium (some low-fat yogurts contain even more than milk) — and it's surprisingly versatile. Enjoy it with fresh fruit for breakfast or add it to soups or sauces instead of cream.

To check the level of fat in the yogurt you buy, read the label. Low-fat yogurt has a butterfat (B.F.) or milk fat (M.F.) content of 2 per cent or less.

*Big Batch Bran Muffins*

## Orange French Toast

**Per Serving:**

Calories: 358

Fat: 12.2 g

Protein: 12.2 g

Carbohydrate: 52.5 g

Calcium: 89 mg

Iron: 2.8 mg

Fiber: 3.8 g

Sodium: 430 mg

Cholesterol: 218 mg

*The subtle orange flavor adds an intriguing taste to this French toast, which is best made with a good multigrain bread. To cut back on fat further, use 1 egg and 1 egg white.*

| 1/4 cup | orange juice | 50 mL |
|---------|-------------|-------|
| 2 | eggs | 2 |
| 1/4 tsp | cinnamon | 1 mL |
| 1 tbsp | margarine or butter | 15 mL |
| 4 | slices whole grain bread | 4 |

**Syrup:**

| 1/2 cup | orange juice | 125 mL |
|---------|-------------|--------|
| 2 tbsp | strawberry jam | 25 mL |

■ In bowl, whisk together orange juice, eggs and cinnamon; set aside.

■ In nonstick skillet, melt half of the margarine or butter over medium heat. Dip bread slices in egg mixture, turning to coat both sides; cook soaked bread, in batches and adding more margarine or butter as necessary, for about 1 minute on each side or until golden brown.

**Syrup:** In small saucepan, combine orange juice with jam; heat, stirring, until jam has melted. Pass separately.

Makes 2 servings.

*Orange French Toast*

**MENU SUGGESTION**

SLICED MELON AND PEACHES

BAKED GRANOLA or JIFFY MUESLI
with MILK
*This Page*

# Baked Granola

**Per Serving:**

Calories: 268

Fat: 11.7 g

Protein: 7.7 g

Carbohydrate: 37 g

Calcium: 39 mg

Iron: 2.5 mg

Fiber: 5.3 g

Sodium: 4 mg

Cholesterol: 0 mg

*Granolas can be very high in fat even though they are very nutritious. Homemade varieties allow you to use less fat and sugar. Sunflower seeds, coconut and nuts all contain fat. Leave one of these out to reduce fat in this recipe. Unsweetened shredded coconut and unsalted sunflower seeds are available at bulk and health food stores.*

| | | |
|---|---|---|
| 3-1/2 cups | rolled oats | 875 mL |
| 1 cup | barley flakes | 250 mL |
| 1 cup | wheat flakes | 250 mL |
| 2/3 cup | natural wheat bran | 150 mL |
| 2/3 cup | oat bran | 150 mL |
| 1/2 cup | wheat germ | 125 mL |
| 1/2 cup | unsalted sunflower seeds | 125 mL |
| 1/2 cup | unsweetened shredded coconut | 125 mL |
| 1/2 cup | sliced almonds | 125 mL |
| 1/3 cup | honey | 75 mL |
| 1/4 cup | vegetable oil | 50 mL |
| 1/2 cup | raisins | 125 mL |

■ In large bowl, mix oats, barley and wheat flakes, wheat and oat bran, wheat germ, sunflower seeds, coconut and almonds. Heat honey and oil until blended; stir into dry ingredients.

■ Spread on baking sheets; bake in 350°F (180°C) oven until lightly browned, stirring twice, about 20 minutes. Add raisins; let cool. Store in airtight container in refrigerator for up to 6 months. Makes 8 cups (2 L), enough for 16 servings.

# Jiffy Muesli

*You can substitute 1-1/2 cups (375 mL) trail mix for the dried apricots, coconut and dates. Trail mix usually has only a small amount of coconut so it is lower in fat.*

| | | |
|---|---|---|
| 3 cups | rolled oats (not instant) | 750 mL |
| 1/2 cup | chopped dried apricots | 125 mL |
| 1/2 cup | flaked coconut | 125 mL |
| 1/2 cup | chopped dates or dried apples | 125 mL |
| 1/2 cup | oat bran | 125 mL |
| 1/2 cup | sunflower seeds | 125 mL |
| 1/2 cup | raisins | 125 mL |
| 1/4 cup | wheat bran | 50 mL |
| 1/4 cup | toasted wheat germ | 50 mL |

**Per Serving:**

Calories: 210

Fat: 6 g

Protein: 7 g

Carbohydrate: 35 g

Calcium: 32 mg

Iron: 2.6 mg

Fiber: 5.6 g

Sodium: 11 mg

Cholesterol: 0 mg

■ Combine rolled oats, apricots, coconut, dates, oat bran, sunflower seeds, raisins, wheat bran and wheat germ; store in airtight container in refrigerator for up to 6 months. Makes 12 servings, each 1/2 cup (125 mL).

**BREAKFAST SMARTS**

■ **Choose high-fiber breakfast foods such as dried or whole fresh fruits instead of juices, and whole grain breads instead of white.**

■ **Use a dash of honey instead of sugar in your cereal or coffee. Because honey is sweeter, you use less.**

■ **Top cereals with natural bran (wheat, oat or corn), wheat germ or fresh fruit.**

■ **Use 2% milk and low-fat yogurt in breakfast favorites to cut down on fat and calories. Changing to 1% milk or skim milk cuts out even more fat and calories.**

■ **Save your breakfast fruit and have it mid-morning in place of a cup of coffee.**

## Orange Yogurt Muffins

**Per Muffin:**

Calories: 191

Fat: 5.2 g

Protein: 4.4 g

Carbohydrate: 32.1 g

Calcium: 76 mg

Iron: 1.2 mg

Fiber: 1.1 g

Sodium: 333 mg

Cholesterol: 21 mg

*Substitute dried apricots for the currants, if desired, in this fine-textured, very orange muffin. To make orange rind strips, use a zester or a cheese grater.*

| 2 cups | all-purpose flour | 500 mL |
|--------|-------------------|--------|
| 1/2 cup | granulated sugar | 125 mL |
| 2 tsp | baking powder | 10 mL |
| 1 tsp | baking soda | 5 mL |
| 1/2 tsp | salt | 2 mL |
| 1/3 cup | currants | 75 mL |
| 1 | egg | 1 |
| 1 cup | low-fat yogurt | 250 mL |
| 1/4 cup | margarine or butter, melted | 50 mL |
| 2 tbsp | orange rind strips | 25 mL |
| 1/4 cup | orange juice | 50 mL |

■ In large bowl, stir together flour, sugar, baking powder, baking soda and salt. Mix in currants.

■ In separate bowl, beat egg; blend in yogurt, margarine or butter, orange rind and juice. Stir into flour mixture just until moistened. Spoon into large greased or paper-lined muffin cups, filling to top. Bake in 350°F (180°C) oven for about 25 minutes or until firm to the touch. Makes 11 muffins.

*Pour-and-Cook Pancakes*

---

**MENU SUGGESTION**

TROPICAL FRUIT SALAD
*Page 120*

ORANGE YOGURT MUFFINS
*This Page*

LIGHT CREAM CHEESE
WITH HONEY OR JAM

---

**MENU SUGGESTION**

POUR-AND-COOK PANCAKES
*This Page*

RASPBERRY FRUIT SAUCE
*Page 118*

BROILED PEAMEAL BACON OR HAM

# Pour-and-Cook Pancakes

**Per Pancake:**

Calories: 130

Fat: 3.4 g

Protein: 4.2 g

Carbohydrate: 20.4 g

Calcium: 103 mg

Iron: 0.9 mg

Fiber: 0.6 g

Sodium: 289 mg

Cholesterol: 21 mg

*Pancakes are simple to make and, in addition to their breakfast role, are one of the original quick suppers. This absolutely reliable pancake recipe is also the basis for the delicious add-ins that follow.*

| | | |
|---|---|---|
| 1 | egg | 1 |
| 2-1/4 cups | 2% milk | 550 mL |
| 2 tbsp | margarine or butter, melted | 25 mL |
| 2 cups | all-purpose flour | 500 mL |
| 2 tbsp | granulated sugar | 25 mL |
| 4 tsp | baking powder | 20 mL |
| 3/4 tsp | salt | 4 mL |
| | Margarine or butter for cooking | |

■ In large bowl, whisk together egg, milk and margarine or butter. In separate bowl, stir together flour, sugar, baking powder and salt; sprinkle over liquid mixture. Stir just enough to moisten.

■ In large skillet, melt just enough margarine or butter over medium to medium-high heat to coat surface of pan. (This is not necessary if using nonstick skillet or griddle.)

■ Pour in 1/4 cup (50 mL) batter at a time for each pancake; cook for 1-1/2 to 2 minutes or until bubbles on top break but do not fill in and pancakes are golden and set on bottoms.

■ Turn and cook for 30 to 60 seconds or until set. Makes 12 pancakes.

## LOW-FAT ADD-INS

Mix these into the basic pancake batter when you add the dry ingredients. (The change in nutrient analysis is negligible.)

### Fresh Berries:
Stir in 3/4 cup (175 mL) blueberries, saskatoons, raspberries or blackberries.

### Dried Fruit:
Stir in 1/2 cup (125 mL) raisins, currants or chopped dates.

### Apricot and Orange:
Stir in 1/2 cup (125 mL) slivered dried apricots and 1 tbsp (15 mL) coarsely grated orange rind.

## FRUIT AND YOGURT SHAKES

You don't need rich ingredients to make a satisfyingly thick milk shake because freezing the fruit gives the same result. Ripe unpeeled bananas can be frozen whole, then peeled and thickly sliced as needed. Or use peeled chopped peaches or mango, or whole frozen strawberries.

■ In blender, combine 1 cup (250 mL) low-fat yogurt, 1/2 cup (125 mL) 2% milk and 2 tsp (10 mL) liquid honey. Add any of the following: 1 cup (250 mL) frozen strawberries, or 2 tbsp (25 mL) frozen raspberry or orange juice concentrate and 1 cup (250 mL) frozen chopped peaches, or 2 tbsp (25 mL) frozen pineapple or orange juice concentrate and one large frozen banana.

■ Process at high speed for 30 to 60 seconds or until smooth and thickened. Makes 1 serving.

*Per Serving (Banana Yogurt Shake): 440 calories, 6.9 g fat, 19.2 g protein, 80.2 g carbohydrate, 614 mg calcium, 0.9 mg iron, 3 g fiber, 235 mg sodium, 24 mg cholesterol.*

# Light Omelette

**Per Serving:**

Calories: 141

Fat: 9.8 g

Protein: 10.4 g

Carbohydrate: 2.1 g

Calcium: 58 mg

Iron: 0.7 mg

Fiber: 0 g

Sodium: 388 mg

Cholesterol: 217 mg

*This light, low-fat omelette should be cooked in a nonstick pan. Add the flavorings and fillings of your choice.*

| | | |
|---|---|---|
| 2 | egg yolks | 2 |
| 2 tsp | vegetable oil | 10 mL |
| 2 tbsp | low-fat yogurt | 25 mL |
| 1/4 tsp | salt | 1 mL |
| | Pepper | |
| 4 | egg whites | 4 |

■ In bowl, whisk egg yolks with 1 tsp (5 mL) of the oil. Stir in yogurt, salt, and pepper to taste.

■ In separate bowl, beat egg whites until soft peaks form; fold into egg yolk mixture until blended.

■ Brush 9-inch (23 cm) nonstick ovenproof skillet with remaining 1 tsp (5 mL) oil; heat over medium-high heat. Add egg mixture and cook for 1-1/2 to 2 minutes or just until top is shiny. Broil for 30 to 45 seconds or until lightly golden. Loosen sides with spatula and slide onto serving plate. Fold omelette over. Makes 2 servings.

## VARIATIONS

### Italian Omelette

Add 2 tbsp (25 mL) freshly grated Parmesan cheese and 1/2 tsp (2 mL) dried oregano to egg yolk mixture. For filling, cook one-quarter sweet red pepper, slivered, 1 slivered hot banana pepper, 2 very thin slices red onion, 1 tsp (5 mL) oil and 1/4 tsp (1 mL) dried oregano until softened. Fold cooked omelette over filling.

*Per Serving (additional ingredients only): 52 calories, 3.9 g fat, 2.4 g protein, 2.2 g carbohydrate, 80 mg calcium, 0.5 mg iron, 0.4 g fiber, 94 mg sodium, 4 mg cholesterol.*

### Cajun Omelette

Before broiling omelette, sprinkle with 1/4 cup (50 mL) shredded Monterey Jack cheese. For filling, combine 1 cup (250 mL) cooked shrimp with 1/3 cup (75 mL) mild or hot salsa. Fold cooked omelette over filling.

*Per Serving (additional ingredients only): 149 calories, 6.8 g fat, 18 g protein, 4 g carbohydrate, 164 mg calcium, 1.6 mg iron, 0 g fiber, 428 mg sodium, 92 mg cholesterol.*

### Mushroom and Ham Omelette

Add 1/2 tsp (2 mL) dried *fines herbes* to egg yolk mixture. For filling, sauté 1 cup (250 mL) thinly sliced mushrooms in 1 tsp (5 mL) oil until softened; combine with 1/2 cup (125 mL) lean chopped ham. Fold cooked omelette over filling.

*Per Serving (additional ingredients only): 78 calories, 4.3 g fat, 7.9 g protein, 1.9 g carbohydrate, 7 mg calcium, 1 mg iron, 0.4 g fiber, 421 mg sodium, 19 mg cholesterol.*

### Greek Omelette

Add 1/2 tsp (2 mL) dried oregano to egg yolk mixture. For filling, combine 1/4 cup (50 mL) chopped black olives, 1/4 cup (50 mL) crumbled feta cheese, 1 large peeled, seeded and chopped tomato, 1/4 cup (50 mL) each chopped sweet green and red peppers. Fold cooked omelette over filling.

*Per Serving (additional ingredients only): 101 calories, 7.3 g fat, 4.2 g protein, 6.1 g carbohydrate, 134 mg calcium, 1.2 mg iron, 1.9 g fiber, 389 mg sodium, 20 mg cholesterol.*

---

### EXCELLENT EGGS

Whether you crack it into an omelette or a fast-and-easy yogurt shake, an egg for breakfast is still a healthy way to start your day.

An economical source of high-quality protein, the egg is a nutrient-rich food. A large egg has about 213 mg of cholesterol and only 5 g of fat — that's just slightly more fat than 1 tsp (5 mL) of margarine or butter. Because the yolk contains all the egg's fat and most of its calories, use one whole egg and one egg white for every two eggs you would normally use in omelettes, scrambled eggs and frittatas.

## Apple Oatmeal

**Per Serving:**

Calories: 201

Fat: 2.6 g

Protein: 6 g

Carbohydrate: 40.9 g

Calcium: 100 mg

Iron: 1.5 mg

Fiber: 4.2 g

Sodium: 167 mg

Cholesterol: 5 mg

*Warm in the tummy, inexpensive porridge provides a nutritious start to the day. The fruit sweetens the oatmeal, so you can eliminate the sugar if desired.*

| | | |
|---|---|---|
| 1 cup | quick-cooking (not instant) rolled oats | 250 mL |
| 1 cup | 2% milk | 250 mL |
| 1 cup | water | 250 mL |
| 1/2 cup | raisins | 125 mL |
| 1 tbsp | (approx) packed brown sugar | 15 mL |
| 1 | apple, chopped | 1 |
| 1/4 tsp | salt | 1 mL |
| | Cinnamon | |

■ In saucepan, mix oats, milk, water, raisins, sugar, apple and salt; bring to boil. Reduce heat to low; cover and simmer, stirring often, for about 10 minutes or until thick and creamy.

■ Dust with cinnamon, and more sugar if desired. Makes 4 servings.

### Microwave method:

■ In 8-cup (2 L) glass measure, combine oats, milk, water, raisins, sugar, apple and salt; microwave, uncovered, at High for 4 to 4-1/2 minutes or just until thickened and creamy, stirring twice. Let stand for 1 minute.

■ Dust with cinnamon, and more sugar if desired. Makes 4 servings.

*Apple Oatmeal*

# Light-Touch Lunches

Lunch is the perfect time to take a break in your busy day with a light yet satisfying meal that's packed with energy and flavor. From Peanut Butter, Carrot and Raisin Sandwiches for the kids to totable Hummus and Grilled Eggplant in Pita or a more elegant Chicken and Spinach Salad with Orange Yogurt Dressing, each easy-to-make recipe in this section has just the right balance of nutrition and appeal to make boring lunches a thing of the past.

## Southwest Stuffed Pepper Plate

**Per Serving:**

Calories: 251

Fat: 10.7 g

Protein: 26.2 g

Carbohydrate: 13 g

Calcium: 187 mg

Iron: 2.3 mg

Fiber: 2.4 g

Sodium: 716 mg

Cholesterol: 70 mg

*Sweet peppers pack a lot of flavor when stuffed with chicken, zucchini and cheese salad. Serve with corn chips and melon slices.*

| | | |
|---|---|---|
| 2 | large sweet green, red or yellow peppers | 2 |
| 3/4 lb | boneless skinless chicken breasts, cooked | 375 g |
| 1 | carrot, julienned | 1 |
| 1 | small zucchini, julienned | 1 |
| 1 | can (4 oz/113 g) green chilies, drained and chopped | 1 |
| 1/2 cup | shredded part-skim-milk mozzarella cheese | 125 mL |
| | Salt and pepper | |
| | Black olives (optional) | |

**Dressing:**

| | | |
|---|---|---|
| 1/2 cup | low-fat yogurt | 125 mL |
| 2 tbsp | light mayonnaise | 25 mL |
| 2 tbsp | taco sauce | 25 mL |
| 2 tsp | chopped fresh coriander or parsley | 10 mL |
| 1 tsp | lime juice | 5 mL |
| 1/4 tsp | dried oregano | 1 mL |
| 2 | green onions, chopped | 2 |
| 1 | clove garlic, minced | 1 |

**Dressing:** Combine yogurt, mayonnaise, taco sauce, coriander, lime juice, oregano, green onions and garlic; set aside.

■ Halve peppers lengthwise; remove seeds and ribs. In steamer over boiling water, steam peppers for 6 to 8 minutes or until tender-crisp. Let cool completely. (Alternatively, arrange, cut sides down, on microwaveable plate in 2 tbsp/25 mL water; cover with vented plastic wrap and microwave at High for 3 to 4 minutes or until tender-crisp, rotating dish twice. Drain off liquid; let cool completely.)

■ Shred chicken into long thin strips. In bowl, toss together chicken, carrot, zucchini, green chilies and cheese; add dressing and toss to coat evenly. Season with salt and pepper to taste. Divide among pepper halves; garnish with olives (if using). *(Stuffed peppers can be covered and refrigerated for up to 1 day.)* Makes 4 servings.

*Southwest Stuffed Pepper Plate*

## Stuffed Tomato Salads

*To prepare tomatoes, slice off tops, scoop out seeds and most of the pulp; sprinkle cavities with salt and invert onto paper towels to drain; chill. Up to an hour before serving, fill with either salad.*

### Dilled Cucumber Salad:

| Per Serving (with tomato): | | | |
|---|---|---|---|
| | 2 | medium cucumbers | 2 |
| Calories: 63 | | Salt | |
| Fat: 1.8 g | 2 tbsp | chopped green onions | 25 mL |
| Protein: 2.6 g | 2 tbsp | chopped fresh parsley | 25 mL |
| Carbohydrate: 11.4 g | 2 tbsp | chopped fresh dill (or 2 tsp/10 mL dried dillweed) | 25 mL |
| Calcium: 56 mg | | | |
| Iron: 1.5 mg | 2 tbsp | low-fat yogurt | 25 mL |
| Fiber: 2.8 g | 1 tbsp | light mayonnaise | 15 mL |
| Sodium: 54 mg | | Pepper | |
| Cholesterol: 2 mg | | | |

■ Peel cucumbers and remove seeds; cut into small strips or cubes. Place in bowl and sprinkle lightly with salt; chill for 1 hour. Rinse in cold water; drain thoroughly. Combine with onions, parsley, dill, yogurt and mayonnaise; season with salt and pepper to taste. Chill for about 1 hour to blend flavors. Makes 3-1/2 cups (875 mL), enough to fill 4 large or 8 small tomatoes, to give 4 servings.

### Seafood Salad with Tarragon:

| Per Serving (with tomato): | | | |
|---|---|---|---|
| | 3 cups | cold cooked shrimp, scallops or fish, cut in bite-size pieces | 750 mL |
| Calories: 174 | | | |
| Fat: 5.5 g | 1/2 cup | chopped celery | 125 mL |
| Protein: 23.1 g | 1/4 cup | chopped green onions | 50 mL |
| Carbohydrate: 9.8 g | 1 tbsp | chopped fresh tarragon (or 1 tsp/5 mL dried) | 15 mL |
| Calcium: 111 mg | | | |
| Iron: 2.7 mg | 2 tbsp | low-fat yogurt | 25 mL |
| Fiber: 2.2 g | 1 tbsp | light mayonnaise | 15 mL |
| Sodium: 204 mg | | Lemon juice | |
| Cholesterol: 122 mg | | Salt and pepper | |

■ Combine shrimp, celery, onions, tarragon, yogurt and mayonnaise. Season to taste with lemon juice, salt and pepper. Chill for about 1 hour to blend flavors. Makes 3-1/2 cups (875 mL), enough to fill 4 large or 8 small tomatoes, to give 4 servings.

## Light Asparagus Crêpes

*Edam cheese, made with partly skimmed 2% milk, is lower in fat than Cheddar or Swiss.*

| | | | |
|---|---|---|---|
| 1/2 lb | fresh asparagus | 250 g |
| 1 cup | 2% milk | 250 mL |
| 3 tbsp | all-purpose flour | 50 mL |
| 1/4 tsp | nutmeg | 1 mL |
| Pinch | white pepper | Pinch |
| 1 cup | shredded Edam cheese | 250 mL |
| 3 tbsp | freshly grated Parmesan cheese | 50 mL |
| 2 | slices back bacon or lean ham, finely chopped | 2 |
| 6 | Low-Fat Crêpes (recipe, p.25) | 6 |

**Per Serving:**

Calories: 194

Fat: 8.7 g

Protein: 13.3 g

Carbohydrate: 15.9 g

Calcium: 274 mg

Iron: 1 mg

Fiber: 1.4 g

Sodium: 395 mg

Cholesterol: 46 mg

■ Cut asparagus into small pieces. In saucepan with 1/2 cup (125 mL) boiling water, cover and cook asparagus for 4 minutes or until tender-crisp. Drain, reserving 1/4 cup (50 mL) of the cooking liquid.

■ In heavy saucepan, whisk together milk, flour, nutmeg and pepper until smooth. Add reserved cooking liquid. Cook over medium-low heat, stirring, for about 5 minutes or until thickened. Stir in Edam cheese until melted.

■ Combine 3/4 cup (175 mL) of the sauce with cooked asparagus, 2 tbsp (25 mL) of the Parmesan cheese and bacon. Divide evenly among crêpes. Fold edges over, envelope-style, to form square package.

■ Place packages, seam side down, in lightly greased 11-×7-inch (2 L) baking dish. Pour remaining sauce over top; sprinkle with remaining Parmesan. Bake in 350°F (180°C) oven for 20 minutes or until heated through. Makes 6 servings.

## Hummus and Grilled Eggplant in Pita

**Per Serving:**

Calories: 467

Fat: 15.8 g

Protein: 13.9 g

Carbohydrate: 71.9 g

Calcium: 102 mg

Iron: 5 mg

Fiber: 11.9 g

Sodium: 772 mg

Cholesterol: 0 mg

*For a delicious sandwich with a difference, fill pita pockets with hummus (a chick-pea spread) and eggplant.*

| | | |
|---|---|---|
| 2 | eggplant (about 3/4 lb/375 g each) | 2 |
| 2 tbsp | vegetable oil | 25 mL |
| 2 tbsp | water | 25 mL |
| 4 | pita rounds (6-inch/15 cm) | 4 |
| | Hummus (recipe follows) | |
| 16 | tomato slices | 16 |
| 8 | lettuce leaves | 8 |

■ Cut eggplant into 16 slices (about 1/4 inch/ 5 mm thick). Combine oil and water; brush over both sides of eggplant slices. Grill on greased rack 4 to 6 inches (10 to 15 cm) from medium-hot coals or on medium-high setting for about 6 minutes per side or until lightly browned and tender.

■ Tear each pita in half and open to form pockets. Spread one side of each pocket with 1/4 cup (50 mL) Hummus; top with 2 eggplant slices, then 2 tomato slices and lettuce leaf. Makes 4 servings (2 halves each).

**Hummus:**

| | | |
|---|---|---|
| 1 tsp | minced garlic | 5 mL |
| 1 | can (19 oz/540 mL) chick-peas, drained | 1 |
| 2 tbsp | tahini (sesame seed paste) | 25 mL |
| 1/4 cup | lemon juice | 50 mL |
| 2 tbsp | water | 25 mL |
| 1/4 tsp | salt | 1 mL |
| Pinch | cayenne pepper | Pinch |

■ In food processor, process garlic and chick-peas until smooth. Add tahini, lemon juice, water, salt and cayenne pepper; process until combined. Makes about 2 cups (500 mL).

*Hummus and Grilled Eggplant in Pita*

## Easy Pita Bread

**Per Large Pita:**

Calories: 172

Fat: 3.8 g

Protein: 4.2 g

Carbohydrate: 29.6 g

Calcium: 8 mg

Iron: 1.6 mg

Fiber: 1 g

Sodium: 298 mg

Cholesterol: 0 mg

*Whether you're packing sandwiches for the back-to-school crowd or making appetizers for a cocktail party, pita bread makes a tasty alternative to the usual fare.*

| 2 cups | warm water | 500 mL |
|---|---|---|
| 1 tsp | granulated sugar | 5 mL |
| 1 | pkg active dry yeast (or 1 tbsp/15 mL) | 1 |
| 5 cups | all-purpose flour | 1.25 L |
| 1/4 cup | vegetable oil | 50 mL |
| 2 tsp | salt | 10 mL |

■ In mixing bowl, combine water and sugar; sprinkle yeast and let stand for 10 minutes or until dissolved and creamy.

■ Using electric mixer, beat in 2 cups (500 mL) of the flour, oil and salt; beat for about 3 minutes or until smooth, scraping down side of bowl from time to time. With wooden spoon, beat in enough of the remaining flour to make stiff dough. Turn out onto lightly floured surface and knead for about 10 minutes or until smooth and elastic.

■ Place dough in lightly greased bowl, turning to grease all over. Cover with plastic wrap and let rise for 1 to 1-1/2 hours or until doubled in bulk.

■ Divide dough into 16 or 32 pieces. On lightly floured surface, roll each piece into 7-inch (18 cm) or 4-inch (10 cm) rounds. Cover and let rise for 15 minutes or until slightly risen. Meanwhile, heat ungreased baking sheet on lowest rack in 500°F (260°C) oven.

■ Using floured metal spatula, quickly transfer 2 or 3 pita rounds to heated baking sheet; bake for 3 to 4 minutes or until puffed and light golden around edges. Repeat with remaining pita rounds.

■ Let cool between damp tea towels. Pitas will collapse and soften slightly but pocket will remain. (Alternatively, if crisp pitas are desired, let cool on racks.) Pitas can be stored in plastic bags in freezer for up to 1 month. Makes 16 7-inch (18 cm) pitas or 32 4-inch (10 cm) pitas.

*Easy Pita Bread*

## Peanut Butter, Carrot and Raisin Sandwiches

*Create a surprise sandwich and stretch the spreading power of peanut butter by adding grated carrot and raisins. And remember that peanut butter plus whole wheat bread add up to a complete protein.*

**Per Serving:**

Calories: 392

Fat: 17.7 g

Protein: 13.8 g

Carbohydrate: 52 g

Calcium: 72 mg

Iron: 2.7 mg

Fiber: 4.3 g

Sodium: 458 mg

Cholesterol: 2 mg

| 1/2 cup | peanut butter | 125 mL |
|---|---|---|
| 1/2 cup | seedless raisins | 125 mL |
| 1/2 cup | grated raw carrots | 125 mL |
| 8 | slices whole wheat bread | 8 |

■ In small bowl, combine peanut butter, raisins and carrots; mix well. Spread over 4 bread slices; top with remaining slices. Wrap in plastic wrap and refrigerate. Makes 4 servings.

### KID-STYLE LUNCHES

Here are 6 easy ways to put pizzazz — *and* food power — into your children's lunches:

**1.** Let children choose their favorite foods from each of the four food groups: milk and milk products, fruits and vegetables, whole grains and breads, and meats or alternates.

**2.** For sandwiches, encourage eating whole grain breads or rolls as well as whole wheat pita. Or pack raisin bran or oatmeal muffins instead.

**3.** Vary sandwich fillings: include sliced cold meat, turkey or chicken, low-fat cheeses and peanut butter. Use canned tuna packed in water instead of oil.

**4.** Pack raw vegetables along with a dip. Make a low-fat dip by adding chopped green onion and parsley to smooth cottage cheese and yogurt. *(Don't forget to pack lunches in an insulated lunch box, along with a frozen box of juice to keep things cool and safe.)*

**5.** For hot foods like chili, baked beans or soup, use a wide-mouth vacuum bottle.

**6.** Include a nutritious sweet such as oatmeal cookies, banana or carrot bread, applesauce or seasonal fruits.

# Light Soufflé

## Per Serving
(without additional ingredients):

Calories: 155

Fat: 9.6 g

Protein: 7.7 g

Carbohydrate: 9.1 g

Calcium: 95 mg

Iron: 0.7 mg

Fiber: 0.2 g

Sodium: 298 mg

Cholesterol: 113 mg

*This light version of a traditional soufflé is lower in calories and fat. For extra flavor and texture, try one of the variations we've suggested.*

|  | Dry bread crumbs |  |
|---|---|---|
| 2 tbsp | margarine or butter | 25 mL |
| 3 tbsp | all-purpose flour | 45 mL |
| 1 cup | 2% milk | 250 mL |
| 1/4 tsp | dry mustard | 1 mL |
| 1/4 tsp | salt | 1 mL |
| Pinch | pepper | Pinch |
| 2 | eggs, separated | 2 |
| 2 | egg whites | 2 |
|  | Additional ingredients (see variations below) |  |
| Pinch | cream of tartar | Pinch |

■ Lightly grease 6-cup (1.5 L) soufflé dish. Dust with bread crumbs; set aside.

■ In small nonstick or heavy saucepan, melt margarine or butter over medium heat. Whisk in flour and cook for 30 seconds. Stir in milk; cook, whisking constantly, for 3 to 5 minutes or until thickened. Remove from heat. Stir in mustard, salt and pepper.

■ Whisk egg yolks; whisk in a little of the sauce. Gradually whisk egg yolk mixture back into pan. Stir in choice of additional ingredients. Set aside.

■ In large bowl, beat egg whites until foamy; beat in cream of tartar until stiff peaks form. Stir one-third into egg yolk mixture. Push remaining whites to one side of bowl. Pour in egg yolk mixture and fold into whites until completely mixed.

■ Pour into prepared soufflé dish. Run finger around soufflé about 3/4 inch (2 cm) from edge. Place on baking sheet and bake in 375°F (190°C) oven for 30 to 35 minutes or until puffed, golden and almost firm to the touch. (Soufflé will rise about 2 inches/5 cm above rim.) Makes 4 servings.

## VARIATIONS

Add to sauce before mixing with egg whites.

### Italian Soufflé

Omit salt and add 1/2 cup (125 mL) shredded part-skim-milk mozzarella cheese, 1/4 cup (50 mL) freshly grated Parmesan cheese, 1/2 cup (125 mL) chopped cooked ham and 1 tsp (5 mL) dried basil.

*Per Serving (additional ingredients only): 238 calories, 14.3 g fat, 16.7 g protein, 10 g carbohydrate, 263 mg calcium, 1 mg iron, 0.2 g fiber, 576 mg sodium, 133 mg cholesterol.*

### Cheese Soufflé

Add 1-1/4 cups (300 mL) shredded Cheddar cheese or half Lappi and half Cheddar, and pinch each nutmeg and cayenne pepper.

*Per Serving (additional ingredients only): 269 calories, 17.4 g fat, 18.3 g protein, 9.8 g carbohydrate, 354 mg calcium, 0.7 mg iron, 0.2 g fiber, 567 mg sodium, 135 mg cholesterol.*

### Asparagus Soufflé

Add 1 cup (250 mL) chopped cooked asparagus, 1/3 cup (75 mL) freshly grated Parmesan or Romano cheese, 1/4 cup (50 mL) soft bread crumbs, pinch nutmeg, and 1/2 tsp (2 mL) grated lemon rind.

*Per Serving (additional ingredients only): 204 calories, 11.8 g fat, 11.9 g protein, 12.6 g carbohydrate, 200 mg calcium, 1.1 mg iron, 1 g fiber, 437 mg sodium, 118 mg cholesterol.*

## AMAZING ASPARAGUS

Fresh, slender spring-green asparagus is one of life's little pleasures — and one of life's little boosts too! One cup (250 mL) of drained cooked pieces contains more vitamin C than half an orange and supplies more than the recommended nutrient intake (30 mg) for an average adult female. As well, it is high in vitamin A — needed for healthy skin and normal bone and tooth development. All that, for only 38 calories and no fat.

*Light Soufflé*

## Pocketful of Greek Salad Plate

*Greek salad is stuffed into whole wheat pita breads for a meal with Mediterranean flavor.*

**Per Serving:**

Calories: 441

Fat: 26.6 g

Protein: 13.4 g

Carbohydrate: 39 g

Calcium: 279 mg

Iron: 3 mg

Fiber: 5.3 g

Sodium: 951 mg

Cholesterol: 39 mg

| | | |
|---|---|---|
| 1/2 cup | thinly sliced red onion | 125 mL |
| 1 cup | diced seedless cucumber | 250 mL |
| 1 cup | drained canned chick-peas, rinsed | 250 mL |
| 1 cup | crumbled feta cheese (about 6 oz/170 g) | 250 mL |
| 1/4 cup | black olives, slivered | 50 mL |
| 1/4 cup | chopped fresh parsley | 50 mL |
| 1 | large tomato, seeded and diced | 1 |
| | Salt and pepper | |
| 4 | 6-inch (15 cm) whole wheat pita breads | 4 |
| 8 | lettuce leaves | 8 |

**Dressing:**

| | | |
|---|---|---|
| 2 tbsp | lemon juice | 25 mL |
| 1/2 tsp | dried oregano | 2 mL |
| 1 | clove garlic, minced | 1 |
| 1/4 cup | olive oil | 50 mL |

**Dressing:** In bowl, whisk together lemon juice, oregano and garlic; gradually whisk in oil. Set aside.

■ In small bowl, soak onion in ice-cold water for 30 minutes; drain and place in large bowl. Add cucumber, chick-peas, cheese, olives, parsley and tomato; add dressing and toss well. Season with salt and pepper to taste.

■ Cut pitas in half and open to form pockets. Line each half with lettuce leaf; spoon in salad. Makes 4 servings.

## Western Omelette in Pita Pockets

**Per Serving:**

Calories: 204

Fat: 9.5 g

Protein: 12.4 g

Carbohydrate: 16.4 g

Calcium: 125 mg

Iron: 1.7 mg

Fiber: 0.7 g

Sodium: 381 mg

Cholesterol: 175 mg

*Crisp fresh greens can be tucked into the pita along with the omelette. Choose red or green leaf lettuce, radicchio, romaine or baby spinach leaves.*

| 1 tsp | butter | 5 mL |
|-------|--------|------|
| 1 tsp | vegetable oil | 5 mL |
| 1/2 cup | sliced mushrooms | 125 mL |
| 2 tbsp | chopped green onion | 25 mL |
| 3 | eggs | 3 |
| 1/2 tsp | dried tarragon | 2 mL |
| | Salt and pepper | |
| 1/2 cup | shredded part-skim-milk mozzarella cheese | 125 mL |
| 1/4 cup | chopped ham | 50 mL |
| 1 tbsp | chopped fresh parsley | 15 mL |
| 2 | 7-inch (18 cm) pita breads, warmed | 2 |

■ In nonstick skillet with heatproof handle, melt butter with oil over medium-low heat; cook mushrooms and onion until mushrooms are softened.

■ Meanwhile, whisk together eggs, tarragon, and salt and pepper to taste. Sprinkle cheese and ham over mushroom mixture; pour in egg mixture, tilting pan to distribute evenly. Cook over medium heat until omelette is set, lifting edges of omelette with spatula and tilting pan to let uncooked mixture flow under. Place under broiler until puffy. Sprinkle with parsley; cut into 4 wedges.

■ Cut each warmed pita in half; tuck omelette wedge into each pocket and serve immediately. Makes 4 servings.

*Western Omelette in Pita Pockets*

# Chicken and Spinach Salad with Orange Yogurt Dressing

**Per Serving:**

Calories: 390

Fat: 12.7 g

Protein: 37.5 g

Carbohydrate: 35 g

Calcium: 323 mg

Iron: 6.2 mg

Fiber: 7.6 g

Sodium: 202 mg

Cholesterol: 77 mg

*Arrange this colorful salad on a platter or on four individual plates.*

| | | |
|---|---|---|
| 1 lb | boneless skinless chicken breasts | 500 g |
| 1/3 cup | orange juice | 75 mL |
| 1 tbsp | vegetable oil | 15 mL |
| 1/2 tsp | grated orange rind | 2 mL |
| 1/3 cup | sliced red onion | 75 mL |
| 8 cups | loosely packed fresh spinach | 2 L |
| 1 | small head radicchio or lettuce | 1 |
| 12 | slices seedless cucumber | 12 |
| 2 | oranges, peeled and sectioned | 2 |
| 8 | dried apricots, quartered | 8 |
| 1/4 cup | toasted sunflower seeds | 50 mL |

**Orange Yogurt Dressing:**

| | | |
|---|---|---|
| 1 cup | low-fat yogurt | 250 mL |
| 2 tbsp | frozen orange juice concentrate | 25 mL |
| 1 tsp | grated orange rind | 5 mL |

**Orange Yogurt Dressing:** Stir together yogurt, orange juice concentrate and rind. Cover and refrigerate.

■ In shallow dish, arrange chicken in single layer. Combine orange juice, oil and orange rind. Pour over chicken; turn to coat all over. Let stand at room temperature for 20 minutes or cover and refrigerate for several hours.

■ Meanwhile, in small bowl, cover onion slices with ice water; refrigerate for 20 minutes.

■ Remove chicken from marinade; broil or grill on greased rack 5 inches (12 cm) from heat for 4 to 5 minutes on each side or until no longer pink inside. Let stand for at least 5 minutes before slicing.

■ Tear spinach and radicchio into bite-size pieces; arrange on serving platter or individual plates. Drain onion slices well. Arrange over spinach mixture along with cucumber, oranges and apricots.

■ Slice chicken breasts diagonally in 1/2-inch (1 cm) wide strips; arrange attractively on salad. Garnish with sunflower seeds. Pass yogurt dressing separately. Makes 4 servings.

# Low-Fat Crêpes

*We've reduced the fat in these crêpes by using one egg white instead of a whole egg. You can reduce fat further by using 1% or skim milk. One crêpe equals one slice of whole wheat bread in nutrients and calories.*

**Per Crêpe:**

Calories: 58

Fat: 1.2 g

Protein: 3 g

Carbohydrate: 9 g

Calcium: 42 mg

Iron: 0.4 mg

Fiber: 0.7 g

Sodium: 25 mg

Cholesterol: 20 mg

| | | |
|---|---|---|
| 1 | egg | 1 |
| 1 | egg white | 1 |
| 1-1/2 cups | 2% milk | 375 mL |
| 1/2 cup | each whole wheat and all-purpose flour | 125 mL |
| Pinch | salt | Pinch |

■ In bowl, lightly beat together egg, egg white and milk. Whisk in whole wheat and all-purpose flours and salt until smooth. Cover and refrigerate for 1 hour.

■ Lightly brush 8-inch (20 cm) nonstick crêpe or omelette pan with oil; heat over medium-high heat. Stir batter and pour 1/4 cup (50 mL) into hot pan, tilting pan to cover bottom evenly. Cook for about 1 minute or until top is dry and no longer sticky. Loosen edge with spatula; slip onto plate. Repeat with remaining batter. *(Crêpes can be wrapped and refrigerated for up to 1 day or frozen for up to 2 months.)* Makes 12 crêpes.

## Baked Potatoes with Two Toppings

**Per Serving (without topping):**

Calories: 230

Fat: 5.9 g

Protein: 3.8 g

Carbohydrate: 41.4 g

Calcium: 18 mg

Iron: 2.2 mg

Fiber: 3.4 g

Sodium: 80 mg

Cholesterol: 0 mg

*Turn easy baked potatoes into a satisfying meal by adding a nutritious topping.*

■ Prick 2 baking potatoes and bake in 400°F (200°C) oven for 45 to 60 minutes. Cut thin slice from tops. Scoop out pulp; mash with 1 tbsp (15 mL) margarine or butter. Season with salt and pepper to taste. Fill skins with potato mixture. Heat in 400°F (200°C) oven for 10 minutes. Add topping if desired. Makes 2 servings.

### Pizza Topping:

| 1/4 cup | each chopped green pepper and onion | 50 mL |
|---------|-------------------------------------|-------|
| 1 tsp | vegetable oil | 5 mL |
| 1/4 cup | tomato sauce | 50 mL |
| 1/4 cup | sliced pepperoni | 50 mL |
| 1/4 cup | shredded part-skim-milk mozzarella | 50 mL |

■ In skillet, cook green pepper and onion in oil over medium-high heat until softened. Top stuffed potatoes with tomato sauce, onion mixture, pepperoni and cheese; broil until cheese melts.

*Per Serving (topping only): 178 calories, 14.1 g fat, 8.6 g protein, 4.6 g carbohydrate, 106 mg calcium, 0.7 mg iron, 0.8 g fiber, 688 mg sodium, 25 mg cholesterol.*

### Virtuous Vegetable Topping:

| 1 cup | broccoli florets | 250 mL |
|-------|------------------|--------|
| 1/2 cup | sliced mushrooms | 125 mL |
| | Low-fat yogurt | |
| | Shredded Cheddar or part-skim-milk mozzarella | |

■ Steam broccoli and mushrooms for 2 minutes or until broccoli is tender-crisp. Top stuffed potatoes with yogurt, broccoli mixture and cheese.

*Per Serving (topping only): 82 calories, 3.6 g fat, 7.6 g protein, 6.4 g carbohydrate, 223 mg calcium, 1.1 mg iron, 2.1 g fiber, 127 mg sodium, 10 mg cholesterol.*

*Baked Potatoes: (bottom left) with Virtuous Vegetable Topping; (top) with Pizza Topping*

**MENU SUGGESTION**

PASTA BEAN SOUP
*This Page*

WHOLE WHEAT PRETZELS
*Page 134*

CRISP VEGETABLE STICKS

MINT-MARINATED FRUIT
*Page 116*

# Cheesy Tortillas

**Per Serving:**

Calories: 286

Fat: 13.9 g

Protein: 13.2 g

Carbohydrate: 27.7 g

Calcium: 275 mg

Iron: 2.2 mg

Fiber: 1.7 g

Sodium: 285 mg

Cholesterol: 39 mg

*These spicy, cheesy tortillas are a snap to make ahead and go well with Fresh Tomato Salsa (recipe, p.101). If Lappi cheese is not available, use a low fat Swiss or mozzarella cheese.*

| | | |
|---|---|---|
| 8 oz | light cream cheese, softened | 250 g |
| 2 cups | shredded Lappi cheese | 500 mL |
| 1 | sweet red pepper, diced | 1 |
| 1/3 cup | chopped green onion | 75 mL |
| 1 tbsp | minced fresh or pickled jalapeño pepper | 15 mL |
| 1 tsp | chili powder | 5 mL |
| 1 tsp | ground cumin | 5 mL |
| 1/2 tsp | pepper | 2 mL |
| 8 | flour tortillas | 8 |

■ In bowl, beat cream cheese until smooth. Blend in Lappi cheese, red pepper, green onion, jalapeño pepper, chili powder, cumin and pepper.

■ Divide filling among tortillas, placing at end of each tortilla. Roll up. Wrap and refrigerate for up to 2 days or freeze for up to 1 month.

■ To heat, wrap individual tortillas in foil; bake in 350°F (180°C) oven for 5 to 8 minutes if refrigerated, 10 to 12 minutes if frozen, or until heated through. (Alternatively, wrap individual tortillas in paper towel and microwave each at High for 30 to 60 seconds or until heated through.) Makes 8 servings.

# Pasta Bean Soup

*This minestrone-like soup makes a terrific one-pot meal. You can substitute any small pasta you have on hand for the shells.*

| | | |
|---|---|---|
| 2 tbsp | vegetable oil | 25 mL |
| 1 | onion, chopped | 1 |
| 1 | carrot, chopped | 1 |
| 1 | stalk celery, chopped | 1 |
| 2 cups | chicken stock | 500 mL |
| 1 | can (19 oz/540 mL) tomatoes (undrained) | 1 |
| 1 | can (19 oz/540 mL) cannellini or white kidney beans (undrained) | 1 |
| 1 tbsp | chopped fresh sage (or 1 tsp/5 mL dried) | 15 mL |
| 1 | bay leaf | 1 |
| 1-1/2 cups | mushrooms, sliced | 375 mL |
| 3/4 cup | pasta shells | 175 mL |
| | Salt and pepper | |
| 1 tbsp | chopped fresh parsley | 15 mL |
| 1/2 cup | freshly grated Parmesan cheese | 125 mL |

**Per Serving:**

Calories: 248

Fat: 7.8 g

Protein: 12.7 g

Carbohydrate: 32.8 g

Calcium: 161 mg

Iron: 2.5 mg

Fiber: 8.5 g

Sodium: 883 mg

Cholesterol: 5 mg

■ In large saucepan, heat oil over medium-high heat; cook onion, carrot and celery for about 5 minutes or until onion is softened.

■ Add chicken stock, tomatoes, beans, sage and bay leaf; bring to boil. Reduce heat to medium-low; cover and simmer for 20 minutes, stirring occasionally and breaking up tomatoes with spoon.

■ Increase heat to medium-high and add mushrooms and pasta; cook, uncovered and stirring occasionally, for about 15 minutes or until pasta is tender. Remove bay leaf; season with salt and pepper to taste. Sprinkle with parsley and Parmesan. Makes 6 servings.

# Soups and Starters

**G**et family meals and entertaining occasions off to a delicious start with this tempting selection of nourishing soups, wholesome breads and low-cal appetizers. Whether it's garden-fresh Tomato and Basil Soup or wholesome Multigrain Bread, each nutritious recipe included here is lower in salt, fat and calories than similar store-bought products — and chock-full of great taste! We've included easy make-ahead directions, timesaving tips and serving suggestions.

## Ginger Squash Soup

**Per Serving:**

Calories: 158

Fat: 5.8 g

Protein: 5.8 g

Carbohydrate: 23.5 g

Calcium: 102 mg

Iron: 2 mg

Fiber: 6.2 g

Sodium: 769 mg

Cholesterol: 2 mg

*Baking or microwaving the squash instead of boiling it helps retain all the flavor. Slowly cooking the leeks over low heat releases their sweetness.*

| | | |
|---|---|---|
| 1 | acorn squash (about 2-1/2 lb/1.25 kg) | 1 |
| 1 tbsp | margarine or butter | 15 mL |
| 1 tbsp | vegetable oil | 15 mL |
| 2 | leeks, thinly sliced | 2 |
| 1 | small carrot, thinly sliced | 1 |
| 4 cups | chicken stock | 1 L |
| 1 tsp | ground ginger | 5 mL |
| 1/2 tsp | salt | 2 mL |
| 1/4 tsp | pepper | 1 mL |
| 1/2 cup | 2% milk | 125 mL |
| | Low-fat yogurt and snipped chives | |

■ Cut squash in half and remove seeds; place cut side down in shallow glass baking dish. Cover and bake in 350°F (180°C) oven for 40 minutes or until tender. (Alternatively, cover with vented plastic wrap and microwave at High for 8 to 10 minutes or until tender. Let stand for 5 minutes.) Scrape squash from skin.

■ Meanwhile, in large saucepan, heat margarine or butter and oil over low heat; cook leeks and carrot, uncovered and stirring occasionally, for about 40 minutes or until leeks are softened and lightly browned. Stir in stock, cooked squash, ginger, salt and pepper; cover and simmer over medium heat for 20 minutes.

■ Transfer to food processor or blender and purée until smooth; return to saucepan. *(Recipe can be prepared to this point, covered and refrigerated for several hours or overnight.)*

■ Stir in milk and heat through but do not boil. Taste and adjust seasoning if necessary. Garnish each serving with swirl of yogurt and sprinkling of chives. Makes 6 servings.

### GARNISHING SOUPS

It's easy to turn a simple soup into a sensational one by adding fresh garnishes. Float thin slices of lemon, zucchini or cucumber on clear soups or sprinkle with alfalfa or bean sprouts, chives or Italian parsley. Make a pattern on puréed or cream soups with finely chopped parsley, or add a dollop of plain yogurt and swirl through the soup for a marbled effect.

*Ginger Squash Soup*

# Hearty Bean Soup

**Per Serving:**

Calories: 374

Fat: 18.3 g

Protein: 25.3 g

Carbohydrate: 27 g

Calcium: 60 mg

Iron: 2.5 mg

Fiber: 7.6 g

Sodium: 741 mg

Cholesterol: 60 mg

*This hearty Portuguese soup, called* Caldo Gallego, *is full flavored with the rich smokiness of chorizo sausage. Serve the soup in warmed bowls along with fresh crusty bread.*

| | | |
|---|---|---|
| 1 tbsp | olive oil | 15 mL |
| 2 | chicken breasts | 2 |
| 1 | onion, chopped | 1 |
| 1 | clove garlic, minced | 1 |
| 2 | potatoes, peeled and cut in 1/2-inch (1 cm) cubes | 2 |
| 8 cups | water | 2 L |
| 1/2 lb | smoked chorizo sausage, thinly sliced | 250 g |
| 1 | can (19 oz/540 mL) red kidney beans, drained and rinsed | 1 |
| 3 cups | shredded cabbage, collards or kale | 750 mL |
| | Salt and pepper | |

■ In large heavy saucepan, heat oil over medium heat; cook chicken for about 7 minutes or until browned all over. Remove and set aside.

■ Add onion and garlic to pan; cook, stirring, for 3 minutes but do not brown. Add potatoes and cook, stirring, for 2 to 3 minutes or until beginning to color.

■ Add water and bring to boil, stirring to scrape up any brown bits from bottom of pan. Return chicken to pan; cover, reduce heat to low and cook for 20 to 25 minutes or until chicken is no longer pink inside.

■ Meanwhile, in skillet, fry sausage over medium-low heat for about 10 minutes or until browned; drain well and reserve. Remove chicken from soup; discard skin and bones. Dice meat and set aside.

■ Add sausage and beans to soup; cover and cook for 5 minutes. Return diced chicken to soup along with cabbage; cook, uncovered, for about 5 minutes or until cabbage is tender. Season with salt and pepper to taste. Makes 6 servings.

# Tomato and Basil Soup

*This copper-hued soup, flecked with green basil, is most flavorful when made with garden-fresh tomatoes. If they're not available, an additional 1 tbsp (15 mL) tomato paste will help boost the flavor of imported tomatoes in wintertime. Freeze any leftover soup for up to 3 months.*

**Per Serving:**

Calories: 137

Fat: 5.3 g

Protein: 5.4 g

Carbohydrate: 18.3 g

Calcium: 35 mg

Iron: 1.4 mg

Fiber: 3 g

Sodium: 603 mg

Cholesterol: 0 mg

| | | |
|---|---|---|
| 3 lb | tomatoes | 1.5 kg |
| 3 tbsp | olive oil | 50 mL |
| 2 | stalks celery, chopped | 2 |
| 1 | parsnip, chopped | 1 |
| 1 | carrot, chopped | 1 |
| 1 | large onion, chopped | 1 |
| 2 | cloves garlic, chopped | 2 |
| 1/2 cup | basmati rice | 125 mL |
| 6 cups | chicken stock | 1.5 L |
| 1/2 cup | fresh basil leaves, torn in pieces | 125 mL |
| 2 tbsp | tomato paste | 25 mL |
| | Salt and pepper | |

■ In large pot of boiling water, blanch tomatoes for 1 minute; plunge into cold water. Remove skins. Chop tomatoes and place in bowl along with juices. Set aside.

■ In large saucepan, heat oil over medium heat; cook celery, parsnip, carrot, onion, garlic and rice, stirring, for about 5 minutes or until onion is softened but not browned.

■ Add stock, tomatoes and half of the basil; simmer, uncovered, for about 40 minutes or until rice and vegetables are tender. Add tomato paste, stirring well; cook for 5 minutes. Stir in remaining basil.

■ In blender or food processor, purée tomato mixture in batches until smooth. Return to saucepan and reheat gently. Season with salt and pepper to taste. Makes 10 1-cup (250 mL) servings.

## Lentil and Lemon Soup

**Per Serving:**

Calories: 304

Fat: 9.8 g

Protein: 20.2 g

Carbohydrate: 35.4 g

Calcium: 68 mg

Iron: 6 mg

Fiber: 6.8 g

Sodium: 1119 mg

Cholesterol: 5 mg

*To lower the sodium in this recipe, use a salt-free chicken stock or vegetable stock.*

| | | |
|---|---|---|
| 6 | slices bacon | 6 |
| 2 tbsp | vegetable oil | 25 mL |
| 3 | carrots, sliced | 3 |
| 2 | stalks celery, sliced | 2 |
| 1 | onion, chopped | 1 |
| 1 | clove garlic, minced | 1 |
| 1-1/2 cups | dried green lentils | 375 mL |
| 6 cups | chicken stock | 1.5 L |
| 1 tsp | grated lemon rind | 5 mL |
| 1 | bay leaf | 1 |
| 1/2 tsp | salt | 2 mL |
| 1/2 cup | chopped fresh parsley | 125 mL |
| 1/4 cup | lemon juice | 50 mL |
| 1 tsp | cumin | 5 mL |

■ In large heavy saucepan, fry bacon over medium-high heat for about 5 minutes or until crisp. Drain on paper towels and let cool; crumble and set aside.

■ Discard all bacon fat in pan and wipe clean. Heat oil in same saucepan and add carrots, celery, onion and garlic; cook over medium heat, stirring often, for 5 minutes or until onion is tender.

■ Rinse lentils and add to pan. Stir in chicken stock, lemon rind, bay leaf and salt; bring to boil. Reduce heat to medium, cover and simmer for 35 to 45 minutes or until lentils are tender. Remove bay leaf. Stir in crumbled bacon, parsley, lemon juice and cumin. Adjust seasoning if necessary. Makes 6 servings.

*Lentil and Lemon Soup*

### LENTILS

**Whether they're red, brown or green, lentils are an amazingly inexpensive source of protein, iron and complex carbohydrates. They're also high in niacin and soluble dietary fiber (the kind found in oat bran).**

# Chunky Gazpacho Soup

**Garnish:**

*Chunky
Gazpacho Soup*

**Per Serving:**

Calories: 37

Fat: 0.3 g

Protein: 1.6 g

Carbohydrate: 8.8 g

Calcium: 20 mg

Iron: 1.2 mg

Fiber: 1.8 g

Sodium: 445 mg

Cholesterol: 0 mg

*You can substitute field cucumbers in this spicy soup, but be sure to seed them.*

| | | |
|---|---|---|
| 3 cups | tomato juice or vegetable cocktail | 750 mL |
| 2 | tomatoes, peeled, seeded and chopped | 2 |
| 1 | sweet red pepper, cut in chunks | 1 |
| 2 cups | chopped peeled English cucumber | 500 mL |
| 1/4 tsp | hot pepper sauce | 1 mL |
| 1/4 tsp | pepper | 1 mL |
| | Salt (optional) | |

| | |
|---|---|
| Chopped cucumber | |
| Chopped sweet yellow and green pepper | |
| Chopped green onion | |

■ In blender or food processor, purée juice, tomatoes, red pepper and cucumber until smooth. Stir in hot pepper sauce, pepper, and salt (if using). To serve, garnish with chopped cucumber, yellow and green pepper and green onion. Makes 6 servings.

## Chunky Fish Soup

**Per Serving:**

Calories: 186

Fat: 3.2 g

Protein: 23.1 g

Carbohydrate: 16.5 g

Calcium: 94 mg

Iron: 2.5 mg

Fiber: 3.1 g

Sodium: 686 mg

Cholesterol: 61 mg

*The flavor of fennel adds Mediterranean flair to this hearty soup.*

| 1 tsp | olive oil | 5 mL |
|-------|-----------|------|
| 1 | clove garlic, minced | 1 |
| 1 | onion, chopped | 1 |
| 1 | can (14 oz/398 mL) tomatoes (undrained) | 1 |
| 2 cups | chicken stock | 500 mL |
| 1 cup | diced potato | 250 mL |
| 1/2 cup | sliced carrot | 125 mL |
| 1/2 cup | sliced celery | 125 mL |
| 2 cups | spinach, torn in bite-size pieces | 500 mL |
| 1 lb | sole fillets, thawed and cut in 1-inch (2.5 cm) cubes | 500 g |
| 1/4 tsp | crushed fennel seeds | 1 mL |
| Dash | hot pepper sauce | Dash |
| | Salt and pepper | |

■ In nonstick Dutch oven, heat oil over medium-low heat; stir in garlic and onion to coat. Add 1 tbsp (15 mL) water. Cover and cook until onion is softened.

■ Add tomatoes, mashing with potato masher. Add chicken stock, potato, carrot and celery; bring to simmer. Cover and cook for 10 minutes or until vegetables are tender.

■ Stir in spinach, sole, fennel seeds, hot pepper sauce, and salt and pepper to taste. Cook, uncovered, just until fish is opaque and flakes easily when tested with fork. Taste and adjust seasoning if necessary. Makes 4 servings.

### Microwave method:

■ In 12-cup (3 L) microwaveable casserole, combine oil, garlic and onion; microwave at High for 1 minute.

■ Add tomatoes, mashing with potato masher. Add chicken stock; cover and microwave at High for 8 to 10 minutes or until boiling. Add potato, carrot and celery; cover and microwave at High for 5 to 8 minutes or until vegetables are tender, stirring once.

■ Stir in spinach, sole, fennel seeds, hot pepper sauce, and salt and pepper to taste; cover and microwave at High for 4 to 6 minutes or until fish flakes easily when tested with fork, stirring once. Let stand, covered, for 5 minutes; taste and adjust seasoning if necessary. Makes 4 servings.

## Minted Green Pea Soup

*Serve this refreshing soup ice-cold. For a variation, omit the mint and serve the soup either chilled or hot (re-heat gently after puréeing).*

**Per Serving:**

Calories: 129

Fat: 3.6 g

Protein: 8.5 g

Carbohydrate: 16.3 g

Calcium: 117 mg

Iron: 2.3 mg

Fiber: 4 g

Sodium: 508 mg

Cholesterol: 3 mg

| 1 tbsp | margarine or butter | 15 mL |
|--------|---------------------|-------|
| 2 | leeks, chopped (white and half of green parts) | 2 |
| 1 | clove garlic, minced | 1 |
| 3 cups | green peas (fresh or frozen) | 750 mL |
| 3 cups | chicken stock | 750 mL |
| 2 cups | packed fresh spinach | 500 mL |
| 2 tbsp | chopped fresh mint | 25 mL |
| 1/2 cup | 2% milk | 125 mL |
| 1/2 cup | low-fat yogurt | 125 mL |
| | Salt and pepper | |

**Garnish (optional):**

| | Low-fat yogurt or chopped mint | |
|--|--|--|

■ In heavy saucepan, melt margarine or butter over medium heat. Add leeks; cover and cook, stirring often, until softened but not browned. Add garlic, peas, chicken stock and spinach; cover and simmer until peas are tender, about 20 minutes. Add mint and simmer for 5 minutes longer.

■ Transfer to food processor or blender and purée until smooth. Add milk, yogurt, and salt and pepper to taste. Chill thoroughly. Garnish each serving with a dollop of yogurt or sprinkle of mint, if desired. Makes 6 servings.

# Golden Harvest Squash Soup

**Per Serving:**

Calories: 163

Fat: 6.7 g

Protein: 4.7 g

Carbohydrate: 23.7 g

Calcium: 40 mg

Iron: 0.9 mg

Fiber: 6 g

Sodium: 434 mg

Cholesterol: 0 mg

*Acorn or butternut squash tastes delicious in this easy-to-make soup, but any fall squash is suitable. For an intriguing presentation, serve soup in acorn squash shells as we have in the photo.*

| 2 tbsp | margarine or butter | 25 mL |
|---|---|---|
| 8 cups | cubed peeled squash (about 3-1/2 lb/1.75 kg) | 2 L |
| 1-1/2 cups | chopped onion | 375 mL |
| 1 cup | chopped peeled apple | 250 mL |
| 2-1/2 cups | chicken stock | 625 mL |
| 1/2 cup | orange juice | 125 mL |
| 1 tsp | ginger | 5 mL |
| 1/2 tsp | salt | 2 mL |
| 1/4 tsp | pepper | 1 mL |
| Dash | hot pepper sauce | Dash |

**Garnish:**

| | Orange slices | |
|---|---|---|
| | Chopped chives | |
| 1 cup | low fat yogurt or light sour cream | 250 mL |

■ In large heavy saucepan, melt margarine or butter over medium heat; cook squash, onion and apple, covered, for about 12 minutes or until slightly softened, stirring occasionally.

■ Stir in stock, orange juice, ginger, salt, pepper and hot pepper sauce; bring to boil. Reduce heat and simmer, covered, for about 15 minutes or until vegetables and apple are tender.

■ Transfer to blender, food processor or food mill; process until puréed. Return to saucepan and heat through if necessary. Taste and adjust seasoning if necessary.

**Garnish:** Ladle soup into warmed bowls; garnish each with orange slice and chives. Pass yogurt or sour cream separately to swirl into soup. Makes 8 appetizer servings.

*Golden Harvest Squash Soup*

# Mushroom, Beef and Barley Soup

*This thick, nourishing soup is reminiscent of grandmother's, but you can make this updated version in minutes. Leftover soup may be refrigerated for up to 4 days.*

| 2 tbsp | margarine or butter | 25 mL |
|---|---|---|
| 2 cups | sliced mushrooms (6 oz/170 g) | 500 mL |
| 1 | clove garlic, minced | 1 |
| 1 tsp | dried marjoram | 5 mL |
| 5 cups | beef stock | 1.25 L |
| 1 | can (14 oz/398 mL) tomato sauce | 1 |
| 2 cups | water | 500 mL |
| 1 | bay leaf | 1 |
| 1 lb | lean ground beef | 500 g |
| 4 | potatoes, cut in 3/4-inch (2 cm) cubes | 4 |
| 3/4 cup | pot or pearl barley | 175 mL |
| 4 cups | spinach, chopped (half 10 oz/284 g pkg) | 1 L |
| | Salt and pepper | |

**Per Serving:**

Calories: 287

Fat: 9.8 g

Protein: 17.2 g

Carbohydrate: 33.8 g

Calcium: 73 mg

Iron: 3.7 mg

Fiber: 4.5 g

Sodium: 886 mg

Cholesterol: 28 mg

■ In large heavy saucepan, melt margarine or butter over medium-high heat; cook mushrooms and garlic for 4 minutes or until softened, stirring often. Sprinkle with marjoram; stir in stock, tomato sauce, water and bay leaf.

■ Meanwhile, in skillet, cook beef over medium-high heat, stirring and breaking up with wooden spoon, for about 5 minutes or until no longer pink. Drain well and add to soup along with potatoes and barley; bring to boil. Reduce heat to medium-low; cover and simmer for 25 to 30 minutes or until potatoes and barley are tender.

■ Stir in spinach; cover and cook for about 4 minutes or just until wilted but still bright green. Remove bay leaf. Season with salt and pepper to taste. Makes 8 servings.

**MENU SUGGESTION**

LIGHT VICHYSSOISE
*This Page*

ORANGE FRENCH TOAST
*Page 10*

SPINACH, WATERCRESS
AND APPLE SALAD
*Page 107*

## Roasted Red Pepper and Tomato Soup

**Per Serving:**

Calories: 78

Fat: 5.2 g

Protein: 2.6 g

Carbohydrate: 6.1 g

Calcium: 21 mg

Iron: 0.9 mg

Fiber: 1.6 g

Sodium: 265 mg

Cholesterol: 0 mg

*Sprinkle shredded mozzarella over top of this richly colored soup.*

| | | |
|---|---|---|
| 2 | large sweet red peppers | 2 |
| 1 | large tomato | 1 |
| 2 tbsp | olive oil | 25 mL |
| 2 cups | chopped onion | 500 mL |
| 2 | cloves garlic, minced | 2 |
| 2 cups | chicken stock | 500 mL |
| 1/4 tsp | dried thyme | 1 mL |
| 1 | bay leaf | 1 |
| 1 tsp | balsamic or red wine vinegar or lemon juice | 5 mL |
| Pinch | cayenne pepper | Pinch |
| | Salt | |

■ On baking sheet, roast red peppers and tomato in 375°F (190°C) oven for about 30 minutes or until puffed and lightly browned. Discard stems and press through food mill or sieve to purée and remove seeds and skin.

■ Meanwhile, in saucepan, heat oil over medium heat; cook onions and garlic, stirring occasionally, for 5 minutes or until onions are translucent.

■ Add stock, thyme, bay leaf and puréed pepper mixture; bring to boil. Reduce heat and simmer, covered, for 20 minutes or until onions are tender. Remove bay leaf. If desired, purée in blender or food processor. Season with vinegar, cayenne pepper, and salt to taste. Makes 6 appetizer servings.

## Light Vichyssoise

*Light cream cheese makes this soup taste creamier and richer than it really is.*

**Per Serving:**

Calories: 157

Fat: 4.6 g

Protein: 6.9 g

Carbohydrate: 22.7 g

Calcium: 43 mg

Iron: 1.3 mg

Fiber: 2.4 g

Sodium: 657 mg

Cholesterol: 11 mg

| | | |
|---|---|---|
| 3 cups | chicken stock | 750 mL |
| 2 cups | diced peeled potatoes (about 2) | 500 mL |
| 1 cup | chopped leeks (white part only, about 2) | 250 mL |
| 2/3 cup | chopped onion | 150 mL |
| 1/4 cup | light cream cheese | 50 mL |
| Pinch | nutmeg | Pinch |
| | Salt and white pepper | |
| | Chopped fresh chives or parsley | |

■ In saucepan, combine stock, potatoes, leeks and onion; bring to boil and cook for 10 minutes or until potatoes are tender.

■ Transfer to food processor or blender. Add cheese and nutmeg; process for 1 to 2 minutes or until smooth. Season with salt and pepper to taste. Serve hot or chilled, garnished with chives. Makes 4 servings.

## Chilled Strawberry and Yogurt Soup

*This refreshing pink soup is pretty served in glass soup bowls.*

**Per Serving:**

Calories: 124

Fat: 2 g

Protein: 5.9 g

Carbohydrate: 22.6 g

Calcium: 196 mg

Iron: 0.6 mg

Fiber: 2.5 g

Sodium: 70 mg

Cholesterol: 6 mg

| | | |
|---|---|---|
| 4 cups | strawberries, hulled | 1 L |
| 2 cups | low-fat yogurt | 500 mL |
| 2 tbsp | liquid honey | 25 mL |
| | Juice of 1 lime | |
| | Mint sprigs | |

■ In food processor or blender, combine strawberries, yogurt, honey and lime juice; purée until smooth.

■ Strain mixture through fine sieve, discarding seeds. Refrigerate for 1 hour. Serve in soup bowls and garnish with sprigs of mint. Makes 5 1-cup (250 mL) servings.

# Multigrain Bread

**Per Slice:**

Calories: 115

Fat: 0.8 g

Protein: 3.2 g

Carbohydrate: 23.6 g

Calcium: 36 mg

Iron: 1.8 mg

Fiber: 1.1 g

Sodium: 210 mg

Cholesterol: 0 mg

*This recipe uses cooked whole grain cereal in combination with all-purpose flour to give a nutritious bread with interesting texture.*

| | | |
|---|---|---|
| 2 cups | water | 500 mL |
| 3/4 cup | multigrain cereal (Red River, 5-grain, 7-grain cereal) | 175 mL |
| 1 tbsp | margarine or butter | 15 mL |
| 1/3 cup | molasses | 75 mL |
| 2 tsp | salt | 10 mL |
| 1 tsp | granulated sugar | 5 mL |
| 1/2 cup | lukewarm water | 125 mL |
| 1 | pkg active dry yeast (or 1 tbsp/15 mL) | 1 |
| 4-1/2 cups | (approx) all-purpose flour | 1.125 L |

■ In saucepan, combine 2 cups (500 mL) water and cereal; bring to boil, stirring frequently. Reduce heat and simmer, stirring occasionally, for about 5 minutes or until slightly thickened. Remove from heat and stir in mar-

garine or butter until melted; stir in molasses and salt. Let cool completely.

■ Dissolve sugar in lukewarm water; sprinkle in yeast and let stand for 10 minutes or until frothy. In large mixing bowl, combine yeast mixture with cereal mixture. Using wooden spoon, gradually beat in enough of the flour to make stiff dough.

■ Turn out dough onto lightly floured surface and knead until smooth and elastic, about 10 minutes. Place in lightly greased bowl, turning to grease all over. Cover with plastic wrap and let rise for 1 to 1-1/2 hours or until doubled in bulk. Punch down dough; turn out onto lightly floured surface and knead into smooth ball. Cover and let rise for 10 minutes.

■ Divide dough in half; shape each portion into loaf and place in greased 8- × 4-inch (1.5 L) loaf pan. Cover and let rise for about 1 hour or until doubled in bulk.

■ Bake loaves in 375°F (190°C) oven for 30 to 35 minutes or until golden brown and loaves sound hollow when tapped on bottoms. Remove from pans and let cool on racks. Makes 2 loaves.

*(top left)*
*Multigrain*
*Bread*

# Persian Flatbreads

**Per Flatbread:**

Calories: 955

Fat: 20.7 g

Protein: 24.1 g

Carbohydrate: 165.4 g

Calcium: 55 mg

Iron: 8.8 mg

Fiber: 5.5 g

Sodium: 1359 mg

Cholesterol: 0 mg

*Sesame seeds make a crisp topping for this soft and chewy flatbread.*

| | | |
|---|---|---|
| 2 tbsp | granulated sugar | 25 mL |
| 2 cups | warm water | 500 mL |
| 1 | pkg active dry yeast (or 1 tbsp/15 mL) | 1 |
| 5 cups | (approx) all-purpose flour | 1.25 L |
| 1/4 cup | margarine or butter, melted | 50 mL |
| 1-1/2 tsp | salt | 7 mL |
| | 2% milk | |
| 2 tbsp | sesame seeds | 25 mL |

■ In large bowl, dissolve sugar in water; sprinkle with yeast and let stand for 10 minutes or until frothy. Using wooden spoon, stir in 3 cups (750 mL) of the flour, margarine or butter, and salt; beat until smooth. Add enough of the remaining flour to form soft dough.

■ Turn out dough onto lightly floured surface; knead for about 10 minutes or until smooth and elastic. Place dough in greased bowl, turning to grease all over. Cover with plastic wrap or damp tea towel; let rise in warm place for about 1-1/4 hours or until doubled in bulk.

■ Punch down dough and divide into 3 portions. Form each portion into ball. Place on lightly floured surface and sprinkle with flour. Cover and let stand for 20 minutes.

■ Stretch and roll out each portion of dough into 16-inch (40 cm) long oval. Place on ungreased baking sheets. Using side of hand, make ridges 1 inch (2.5 cm) apart down length of each oval. Brush each loaf with milk and sprinkle with sesame seeds. Let stand for 15 minutes. Bake in 375°F (190°C) oven for 25 to 30 minutes or until golden brown. Remove from baking sheets and let cool on wire racks. Makes 3 large flatbreads (each flatbread serves 4 to 6, depending on use).

# Armenian Flatbreads

*This crackerlike bread is perfect with pâtés, dips and creamy cheeses.*

| | | |
|---|---|---|
| 1/2 cup | warm water | 125 mL |
| 4 | egg whites | 4 |
| 1 tbsp | margarine or butter, melted | 15 mL |
| 1 tsp | salt | 5 mL |
| 1 tsp | granulated sugar | 5 mL |
| 1 tsp | active dry yeast | 5 mL |
| 2-1/2 cups | (approx) all-purpose flour | 625 mL |
| 1 tbsp | each sesame and poppy seeds | 15 mL |

**Per Flatbread:**

Calories: 352

Fat: 5.9 g

Protein: 12.7 g

Carbohydrate: 60.7 g

Calcium: 55 mg

Iron: 3.5 mg

Fiber: 2.1 g

Sodium: 658 mg

Cholesterol: 0 mg

■ In bowl, combine water, egg whites, margarine or butter, salt, sugar and yeast. Using wooden spoon, stir in 2 cups (500 mL) of the flour; beat until smooth. Add enough of the remaining flour to form soft dough.

■ Turn out dough onto lightly floured surface; knead several times or until dough holds together. Place dough in greased bowl, turning to grease all over. Cover with plastic wrap or damp tea towel and let rise in warm place for about 1-1/4 hours or until doubled in bulk.

■ Punch down dough and turn out onto lightly floured surface. Divide into 4 portions. Roll out each portion into 1/8-inch (3 mm) thick circle. Place on lightly greased baking sheets. Prick dough all over with fork. Brush lightly with water; sprinkle with sesame and poppy seeds. Bake in 400°F (200°C) oven for about 15 minutes or until golden brown. Remove from baking sheets and let cool on wire racks. Makes 4 large flatbreads (8 appetizer servings each).

## Corn Bread

**Per Serving:**

Calories: 256

Fat: 11 g

Protein: 9.1 g

Carbohydrate: 29.7 g

Calcium: 165 mg

Iron: 1.1 mg

Fiber: 1.3 g

Sodium: 462 mg

Cholesterol: 64 mg

*For extra flavor, add 2 tbsp (25 mL) drained and chopped canned chili peppers and 1/4 tsp (1 mL) dried oregano before pouring batter into pan.*

| 1 cup | all-purpose flour | 250 mL |
|---|---|---|
| 1-1/2 tsp | baking powder | 7 mL |
| 1 tsp | baking soda | 5 mL |
| 1/2 tsp | salt | 2 mL |
| 1 cup | cornmeal | 250 mL |
| 1 cup | shredded Lappi cheese | 250 mL |
| 2 | eggs | 2 |
| 1 cup | buttermilk | 250 mL |
| 1/4 cup | vegetable oil | 50 mL |
| 1 tbsp | liquid honey | 15 mL |

■ In large bowl, stir together flour, baking powder, baking soda and salt; stir in cornmeal and cheese. In separate bowl, beat together eggs, buttermilk, oil and honey; stir into dry ingredients just until blended.

■ Pour into greased and floured 8-inch (2 L) square cake pan. Bake in 425°F (220°C) oven for 20 to 25 minutes or until cake tester inserted in center comes out clean. Makes 8 servings.

*(bottom right) Armenian Flatbreads; (top right) Persian Flatbreads*

## Mexican Bean Dip

**Per Tbsp (15 mL):**

Calories: 28

Fat: 1.4 g

Protein: 1.2 g

Carbohydrate: 2.9 g

Calcium: 20 mg

Iron: 0.3 mg

Fiber: 0.7 g

Sodium: 93 mg

Cholesterol: 1 mg

*Since refried beans are high in fat, we've used canned pinto beans.*

| | | |
|---|---|---|
| 2 tbsp | vegetable oil | 25 mL |
| 1 | tomato, peeled, seeded and chopped | 1 |
| 1/2 cup | chopped onion | 125 mL |
| 1/3 cup | canned diced green chilies | 75 mL |
| 1 | can (14 oz/398 mL) pinto beans (undrained) | 1 |
| 1 tsp | lime juice | 5 mL |
| 2 tsp | chili powder | 10 mL |
| | Pepper | |
| 1/4 cup | low-fat yogurt | 50 mL |
| 2 tbsp | finely chopped fresh parsley | 25 mL |
| 1 tbsp | minced onion | 15 mL |

**Garnish:**

| | | |
|---|---|---|
| 1 | green onion, thinly sliced | 1 |
| 2 tbsp | grated Monterey Jack cheese | 25 mL |

■ In skillet, heat oil over medium-high heat; cook tomato, onion and chilies, stirring often, until onion is softened and liquid has evaporated.

■ Add beans, mashing with potato masher; cook, stirring, for about 2 minutes or until consistency of coarse purée. Transfer to bowl. Stir in lime juice, chili powder, and pepper to taste; cover and refrigerate until cool. Stir in yogurt, parsley and minced onion. Refrigerate, covered, until serving time. Garnish with green onion and cheese. Makes 1-3/4 cups (425 mL).

### DRAINED YOGURT

**For dips that will retain a creamy texture, strain yogurt through a cloth-lined sieve before measuring. Refrigerate for at least 1 hour to allow any excess liquid to drain away.**

## Orange and Red Onion Dip

*This dip goes well with cucumber, endive leaves and carrot sticks. For added color on the plate, pat cooked tiny beets dry and spear with cocktail picks or bamboo skewers for dipping.*

| | | |
|---|---|---|
| 3/4 cup | drained low-fat yogurt (see sidebar below) | 175 mL |
| 1/2 cup | light mayonnaise | 125 mL |
| 1/4 cup | finely chopped red onion | 50 mL |
| 1 tsp | grated orange rind | 5 mL |
| 1 tsp | finely chopped fresh mint | 5 mL |
| | White pepper | |

**Per Tbsp (15 mL):**

Calories: 24

Fat: 2 g

Protein: 0.5 g

Carbohydrate: 1.2 g

Calcium: 17 mg

Iron: 0 mg

Fiber: 0 g

Sodium: 59 mg

Cholesterol: 4 mg

■ In bowl, stir together yogurt and mayonnaise. Stir in onion, orange rind, mint, and pepper to taste. Cover and refrigerate for at least 1 hour or up to 12 hours. Makes 1-1/4 cups (300 mL).

## Fresh Mango and Chutney Dip

*This tangy sweet dip goes well with raw vegetables and fruit, baby corn or cherry tomatoes.*

| | | |
|---|---|---|
| 1/2 cup | drained low-fat yogurt (see sidebar this page) | 125 mL |
| 2 tbsp | light mayonnaise | 25 mL |
| 1/3 cup | finely chopped peeled mango | 75 mL |
| 2 tbsp | chutney | 25 mL |
| Dash | hot pepper sauce | Dash |

**Per Tbsp (15 mL):**

Calories: 13

Fat: 0.7 g

Protein: 0.5 g

Carbohydrate: 1.4 g

Calcium: 15 mg

Iron: 0 mg

Fiber: 0.1 g

Sodium: 30 mg

Cholesterol: 1 mg

■ In bowl, stir together yogurt and mayonnaise. Stir in mango, chutney and hot pepper sauce. Cover and refrigerate for at least 1 hour or up to 12 hours. Makes 1 cup (250 mL).

# Spicy Shrimp with Dipping Sauces

**Per Serving:**

Calories: 132

Fat: 6.7 g

Protein: 15.9 g

Carbohydrate: 2.9 g

Calcium: 63 mg

Iron: 1.9 mg

Fiber: 0.6 g

Sodium: 124 mg

Cholesterol: 88 mg

*For this special appetizer, use jumbo shrimp that have been lightly cooked and peeled (with the tail left on).*

| 1 lb | jumbo shrimp | 500 g |
|------|--------------|-------|
| 1 tbsp | chili powder | 15 mL |
| 1-1/2 tsp | paprika | 7 mL |
| 1/2 tsp | cumin | 2 mL |
| Pinch | each salt and cayenne pepper | Pinch |
| 1 tbsp | vegetable oil | 15 mL |
| | Dipping Sauces (recipes follow) | |

■ Combine chili powder, paprika, cumin, salt and cayenne; set aside.

■ In large nonstick skillet, heat oil over high heat. Add shrimp and sauté for 1 minute.

Sprinkle with spice mixture; cook, stirring, for 2 minutes longer or just until very hot. Serve hot with dipping sauces. Makes 4 servings.

## Cool Cucumber Dipping Sauce:

■ Combine 3/4 cup (175 mL) low-fat yogurt, 1 cup (250 mL) finely chopped seedless cucumber, 2 tbsp (25 mL) chopped chives or mint, and salt and pepper to taste. Makes 1-1/2 cups (175 mL).

*Per Tbsp (15 mL): 33 calories, 0.8 g fat, 2.6 g protein, 4 g carbohydrate, 88 mg calcium, 0.1 mg iron, 0.2 g fiber, 33 mg sodium, 3 mg cholesterol.*

## Tomato Salsa:

■ Combine 1 cup (250 mL) crushed canned tomatoes, 1/4 cup (50 mL) each minced onion and sweet red pepper, 2 minced cloves garlic, and salt and pepper to taste. Makes 1-1/2 cups (175 mL).

*Per Tbsp (15 mL): 19 calories, 0.2 g fat, 0.8 g protein, 4 g carbohydrate, 21 mg calcium, 0.5 mg iron, 0.9 g fiber, 98 mg sodium, 0 mg cholesterol.*

*Spicy Shrimp with Dipping Sauces*

**MENU SUGGESTION**

GOAT CHEESE, SPINACH AND
MUSHROOM DIP
*This Page*

CRUDITÉS

COUSCOUS PILAF
*Page 93*

GRILLED LEMON AND ROSEMARY CHICKEN
*Page 60*

# Goat Cheese, Spinach and Mushroom Dip

*Look for goat cheese with a fat content of less than 20%.*

| | | |
|---|---|---|
| 1/3 cup | goat cheese | 75 mL |
| 2 tbsp | light mayonnaise | 25 mL |
| 1/4 cup | buttermilk | 50 mL |
| 2 tsp | prepared horseradish | 10 mL |
| | Nutmeg | |
| | Pepper | |
| 1/3 cup | finely chopped mushrooms | 75 mL |
| 1/4 cup | finely chopped fresh spinach | 50 mL |

**Per Tbsp (15 mL):**

Calories: 22

Fat: 1.7 g

Protein: 0.9 g

Carbohydrate: 0.7 g

Calcium: 32 mg

Iron: 0.1 mg

Fiber: 0.1 g

Sodium: 80 mg

Cholesterol: 6 mg

■ In bowl, stir together cheese and mayonnaise until smooth. Gradually whisk in buttermilk. Stir in horseradish, and nutmeg and pepper to taste. Stir in mushrooms and spinach. *(Dip can be covered and refrigerated for up to 8 hours.)* Makes 1 cup (250 mL).

# Tortellini Skewers

**Per Serving:**

Calories: 34

Fat: 1.5 g

Protein: 1.2 g

Carbohydrate: 4 g

Calcium: 2 mg

Iron: 0.1 mg

Fiber: 0.2 g

Sodium: 35 mg

Cholesterol: 2 mg

*Green and white tortellini filled with meat or cheese filling make fabulous appetizers. Thread different colors of the tortellini onto wooden skewers, then arrange them with crudités around one or several dips on a serving plate. Increase the amount of tortellini for a crowd. They're delicious served either warm or at room temperature.*

| | | |
|---|---|---|
| 1/2 lb | tortellini* | 250 g |
| 1 tbsp | olive oil | 15 mL |
| | Goat Cheese, Spinach and Mushroom Dip (recipe, this page) | |

■ In large pot of boiling water, cook tortellini according to package directions or until pasta is tender but firm. Drain and return to pot; toss with oil to prevent sticking.

■ Thread 2 tortellini, 1 of each color, onto each skewer. *(Skewers can be covered and refrigerated for up to 1 day. To serve, bring to room temperature or reheat by dipping into boiling water.)*

■ Set dip in center of platter; surround with skewers. Makes 25 hors d'oeuvres.

*Available in frozen food and dairy sections of most supermarkets.

# Smoked Trout Pâté

*For quick canapés, spread pâté on melba toast or thick cucumber, white turnip or carrot slices.*

| | | |
|---|---|---|
| 1/3 lb | smoked trout, skinned and boned | 175 g |
| 1 cup | low-fat cottage cheese | 250 mL |
| 4 oz | light cream cheese | 125 g |
| 1 tbsp | lemon juice | 15 mL |
| 2 tsp | minced onion | 10 mL |
| 2 tsp | chopped fresh dill or parsley | 10 mL |
| 1/4 tsp | hot pepper sauce | 1 mL |

**Per Tbsp (15 mL):**

Calories: 45

Fat: 2.9 g

Protein: 4.4 g

Carbohydrate: 0.8 g

Calcium: 13 mg

Iron: 0.2 mg

Fiber: 0 g

Sodium: 679 mg

Cholesterol: 10 mg

■ In food processor, combine smoked trout, cottage cheese, cream cheese, lemon juice, onion, dill and hot pepper sauce; process for about 2 minutes or until puréed and smooth. Spoon into serving crock or dish. Cover and refrigerate until chilled. Makes 1-1/2 cups (375 mL).

# Bruschetta

**Per Serving:**

Calories: 127

Fat: 3.8 g

Protein: 3.5 g

Carbohydrate: 20.3 g

Calcium: 15 mg

Iron: 1.2 mg

Fiber: 1.6 g

Sodium: 173 mg

Cholesterol: 0 mg

*This easy no-fuss appetizer is as tempting to look at as it is to eat. It's ideal as a first course any time of year.*

| | | |
|---|---|---|
| 2 tbsp | olive oil | 25 mL |
| 4 | cloves garlic, minced | 4 |
| 1 | Italian ring loaf, about 12 inches (30 cm) in diameter | 1 |
| 4 | large tomatoes, peeled, seeded and chopped | 4 |
| 2 tbsp | finely shredded fresh basil | 25 mL |
| | Salt and pepper | |

■ In small nonstick skillet, heat oil over medium-low heat; cook garlic for 3 minutes or until softened.

■ Slice loaf horizontally; reserve one half for another use. Brush cut side of remaining half with some of the garlic-oil mixture. Broil on baking sheet until golden brown.

■ Meanwhile, toss together tomatoes, basil, remaining garlic-oil mixture, and salt and pepper to taste. Spoon over loaf; cut into thick wedges to serve. Makes 8 servings.

*Tortellini Skewers*

43

# Mussels with Curry Sauce

## Per Serving:

Calories: 96

Fat: 3.2 g

Protein: 9.6 g

Carbohydrate: 7 g

Calcium: 157 mg

Iron: 2 mg

Fiber: 0.3 g

Sodium: 168 mg

Cholesterol: 25 mg

*Here's a tasty make-ahead way to serve mussels as an hors d'oeuvre. For a crowd, make several batches and include the variations given below.*

| 1 cup | water | 250 mL |
|-------|-------|--------|
| 24 | mussels, cleaned and beards removed | 24 |
| 1 tsp | vegetable oil | 5 mL |
| 1 tbsp | curry powder | 15 mL |
| 1 cup | low-fat yogurt | 250 mL |
| 1 tbsp | lime juice | 15 mL |
| | Salt and pepper | |

■ In large pot over high heat, bring water to boil; add mussels, discarding any that are not closed. Cover and steam until shells open, about 5 minutes; drain, discarding any that have not opened. Remove mussels from shells, reserving shells.

■ Meanwhile, in small skillet, heat oil; add curry powder and cook gently until aromatic. Remove from heat and blend in yogurt, lime juice, and salt and pepper to taste.

■ Spoon sauce over mussels; cover and marinate in refrigerator for 24 hours. To serve, spoon mussels back into shells. Spoon marinade over top. Makes 4 servings.

### Mussels with Tarragon Tartare:

| 1 tbsp | tarragon vinegar | 15 mL |
|--------|------------------|-------|
| 1 tbsp | chopped dill pickle | 15 mL |
| 1 tsp | dried tarragon | 5 mL |
| 1 tsp | chopped capers | 5 mL |
| 1 tsp | Dijon mustard | 5 mL |
| 1/4 cup | low-fat yogurt or buttermilk | 50 mL |
| 1/4 cup | light mayonnaise | 50 mL |
| 1 tbsp | chopped fresh parsley | 15 mL |
| | Salt and pepper | |

■ In small bowl, combine vinegar, dill pickle, tarragon, capers and mustard; stir in yogurt and mayonnaise. Add parsley; season with salt and pepper to taste. Spoon sauce over mussels; cover and marinate in refrigerator for 24 hours. Makes 4 servings.

*Per Serving: 95 calories, 5.8 g fat, 7 g protein, 3.6 g carbohydrate, 63 mg calcium, 1.7 mg iron, 0.1 g fiber, 322 mg sodium, 29 mg cholesterol.*

### Mussels with Light Vinaigrette:

| 2 tbsp | Balsamic vinegar | 25 mL |
|--------|------------------|-------|
| 1 tsp | Dijon mustard | 5 mL |
| 2 tbsp | olive oil | 25 mL |
| 1/4 cup | chopped fresh chives | 50 mL |
| | Salt and pepper | |

■ In small bowl, whisk together vinegar and mustard; gradually whisk in oil. Stir in chives. Season with salt and pepper to taste. Spoon sauce over mussels; cover and marinate in refrigerator for 24 hours. Makes 4 servings.

*Per Serving: 103 calories, 7.7 g fat, 6.3 g protein, 2 g carbohydrate, 42 mg calcium, 1.6 mg iron, 0.1 g fiber, 141 mg sodium, 21 mg cholesterol.*

# Chicken Pinwheels

**Per Slice:**

Calories: 35

Fat: 0.8 g

Protein: 4.9 g

Carbohydrate: 2.1 g

Calcium: 14 mg

Iron: 0.3 mg

Fiber: 0.2 g

Sodium: 40 mg

Cholesterol: 12 mg

*These delicious chicken rolls, which keep in the refrigerator for up to 3 days, make 24 appetizers or 4 main-dish servings.*

| | | |
|---|---|---|
| 4 | boneless skinless chicken breasts | 4 |
| 1 cup | finely chopped cooked broccoli | 250 mL |
| 1/2 cup | whole wheat bread crumbs | 125 mL |
| 1 | clove garlic, minced | 1 |
| 1 tbsp | chopped fresh basil | 15 mL |
| 2 tsp | chopped walnuts | 10 mL |
| 2 tsp | soy sauce | 10 mL |
| | Pepper | |
| 1 tsp | rice vinegar or lemon juice | 15 mL |
| | Paprika | |

■ Pound chicken to 1/4-inch (5 mm) thickness.

■ In bowl, combine broccoli, crumbs, garlic, basil, walnuts, soy sauce, and pepper to taste. Spread evenly over each breast. Roll up from short end, jelly-roll style. Brush rolls with vinegar; sprinkle with paprika.

■ Place rolls seam side down in nonstick baking pan. Bake in 325°F (160°C) oven for 30 minutes or until chicken is no longer pink inside. Let cool; cover and chill. Cut into 1/2-inch (1 cm) thick slices. Makes 24 slices.

---

**WHAT'S IN A MUSSEL?**

Mussels aren't just tasty and economical. They're nutritious too — high in protein and minerals and low in fat and cholesterol. When buying fresh mussels, look for clean, shiny, bluish or brownish black shells. Test mussels to make sure they are alive by tapping opened shells firmly. Discard any that do not close. After cooking, discard any that remain closed.

---

# Flank Steak Roll-ups

*These attractive roll-ups make wonderful appetizers in both taste and presentation.*

**Per Roll-up:**

Calories: 38

Fat: 1.5 g

Protein: 5 g

Carbohydrate: 1.3 g

Calcium: 10 mg

Iron: 0.5 mg

Fiber: 0.4 g

Sodium: 198 mg

Cholesterol: 8 mg

| | | |
|---|---|---|
| 1-1/2 lb | flank steak | 750 g |
| 2 | bunches broccoli | 2 |
| 1 tbsp | lemon juice | 15 mL |
| | Pepper | |

**Marinade:**

| | | |
|---|---|---|
| 1/2 cup | soy sauce | 125 mL |
| 1/2 cup | water | 125 mL |
| 1 tsp | grated lemon rind | 5 mL |
| 2 tbsp | lemon juice | 25 mL |
| 1 | clove garlic, minced | 1 |
| 1 tsp | dried thyme | 5 mL |
| | Pepper | |

**Marinade:** Mix together soy sauce, water, lemon rind, lemon juice, garlic, thyme, and pepper to taste. Place steak in large shallow dish; pour marinade over and marinate at room temperature for 2 hours, turning once.

■ Meanwhile, divide broccoli into florets (use stalks for vegetable dip or soup). In large pot of boiling water, cook florets for 2 minutes. Drain and immerse in cold water until cold; drain well and pat dry. Sprinkle with lemon juice, and pepper to taste.

■ Drain steak and broil for 3 minutes on each side or until desired doneness. Let cool and slice across the grain into very thin strips. Roll each strip tightly around broccoli floret and arrange on serving plate. Makes 36 appetizers.

# Marvelous Main Dishes

These meat, fish and pasta main dishes are totally in step with today's trend to lighter, healthier eating. We've kept fat to a minimum and suggested cooking methods like broiling, grilling, roasting or stir-frying that keep meat and fish naturally tender and moist. The addition of herbs and spices enhances the great taste of dishes without increasing calories or salt. And we've teamed smaller, better-for-you portions with fresh vegetables and high-energy carbohydrates like rice, potatoes and whole grain breads.

## Lamb Curry

**Per Serving:**

Calories: 314

Fat: 14.4 g

Protein: 29.5 g

Carbohydrate: 16.9 g

Calcium: 72 mg

Iron: 3.5 mg

Fiber: 3.4 g

Sodium: 250 mg

Cholesterol: 102 mg

*Choose long grain brown or white rice or a Basmati or other aromatic rice to serve with this curry.*

| | | |
|---|---|---|
| 2 lb | boneless lamb shoulder, trimmed and cut in 1-inch (2.5 cm) cubes | 1 kg |
| 1 tbsp | all-purpose flour | 15 mL |
| 1 tbsp | vegetable oil | 15 mL |
| 1 | large onion, finely chopped | 1 |
| 1 | stalk celery, chopped | 1 |
| 1 | carrot, diced | 1 |
| 2 | cloves garlic, minced | 2 |
| 1 tsp | minced gingerroot | 5 mL |
| 4 tsp | curry powder | 20 mL |
| 1 tsp | coriander seeds, crushed | 5 mL |
| 1 | can (14 oz/398 mL) tomatoes (undrained), crushed | 1 |
| 1/4 cup | chicken stock or tomato juice | 50 mL |
| 1 | apple, peeled, cored and chopped | 1 |
| | Salt and pepper | |

■ Toss lamb with flour. In nonstick Dutch oven or large saucepan, heat oil over high heat; cook lamb, turning often, until browned on all sides. Pour off any fat.

■ Reduce heat to medium. Add onion, celery, carrot, garlic and gingerroot; cover and cook for 3 to 4 minutes or until onion is softened. Add curry powder and coriander seeds; cook for 2 minutes.

■ Add tomatoes and chicken stock; bring to simmer. Reduce heat to medium-low; cover and cook, stirring occasionally, for 10 minutes. Add apple; cook for 15 to 20 minutes or until lamb is tender. Season with salt and pepper to taste. Makes 4 servings.

### WHICH COOKING OIL IS BEST?

Look for and use oils that are good sources of polyunsaturated and monounsaturated fats — canola, safflower, sunflower, corn and olive oil are good choices — and let your recipe dictate which ones to use when. The robust flavor of olive oil is suited to heartier dishes, while the other oils are better in delicately flavored recipes. But whatever the oil, remember to treat it as a fat and to use it sparingly.

*Lamb Curry*

## Herbed Flank Steak

| 1 tbsp | vegetable oil | 15 mL |
| | Salt | |

*Herbed Flank Steak*

**Per Serving:**

Calories: 241

Fat: 13.7 g

Protein: 26.3 g

Carbohydrate: 1.3 g

Calcium: 18 mg

Iron: 2.2 mg

Fiber: 0.2 g

Sodium: 57 mg

Cholesterol: 47 mg

*For this recipe, purchase flank steak that has not been scored by the butcher. Too many scorings will make meat difficult to carve.*

| 1 lb | flank steak, trimmed | 500 g |
| 1/3 cup | chopped onion | 75 mL |
| 1/4 cup | dry white wine | 50 mL |
| 2 tbsp | chopped fresh parsley | 25 mL |
| 2 tbsp | each chopped fresh oregano and thyme (or 2 tsp/10 mL dried) | 25 mL |
| 1 tbsp | olive oil | 15 mL |
| 1 tbsp | lemon juice | 15 mL |
| 1 | bay leaf | 1 |
| 2 | cloves garlic, minced | 2 |
| 1/4 tsp | each dry mustard and pepper | 1 mL |

■ Score steak with 8 diagonal slashes about 1/8 inch (3 mm) deep. Place in shallow glass dish. Combine onion, wine, parsley, oregano, thyme, olive oil, lemon juice, bay leaf, garlic, mustard and pepper; spoon over meat, turning to coat. Cover and refrigerate for at least 2 hours or overnight, turning meat occasionally. Remove steak from marinade; pat steak dry.

■ Brush grill with oil. Grill steak over medium-hot coals, or broil, for 5 to 7 minutes per side for medium-rare or until desired doneness. (Alternatively, heat browning grill according to manufacturer's instructions; add oil and tilt to coat evenly. Press steak onto grill; microwave at High for 1 minute. Turn and microwave for 1 to 2 minutes longer for rare or until desired doneness.) Season with salt to taste. To serve, thinly slice across the grain diagonally. Makes 4 servings.

# Hamburger Skillet Supper

**Per Serving:**

Calories: 324

Fat: 9.4 g

Protein: 21.2 g

Carbohydrate: 39.4 g

Calcium: 97 mg

Iron: 3.6 mg

Fiber: 5.7 g

Sodium: 431 mg

Cholesterol: 37 mg

*Prepare a dinner completely in one skillet. Round out the menu with a dark pumpernickel or rye bread and fresh fruit wedges for dessert.*

| | | |
|---|---|---|
| 1 lb | lean ground beef | 500 g |
| 1 | Spanish onion, coarsely chopped | 1 |
| 1 | sweet green pepper, coarsely chopped | 1 |
| 1 | large stalk celery, thinly sliced | 1 |
| 4 | carrots, thinly sliced | 4 |
| 1 | can (28 oz/796 mL) tomatoes (undrained) | 1 |
| 1 cup | beef stock | 250 mL |
| 2 tsp | paprika | 10 mL |
| 1 tsp | dried oregano | 5 mL |
| 1/2 tsp | cinnamon | 2 mL |
| 1-1/2 cups | penne or other short pasta | 375 mL |
| 2 cups | coarsely shredded cabbage | 500 mL |
| | Salt and pepper | |

■ In large nonstick skillet or Dutch oven, cook beef over medium-high heat, stirring to break up, until browned; drain off excess fat. Add onion, green pepper, celery and carrots; cook, stirring occasionally, until onion is softened.

■ Add tomatoes, beef stock, paprika, oregano and cinnamon, breaking up tomatoes with fork; bring to simmer. Stir in pasta; cover and cook for 10 to 12 minutes or until pasta is tender but firm. Add cabbage; cover and cook for 3 to 5 minutes or just until tender. Season with salt and pepper to taste. Makes 6 servings.

> **Ground beef is inexpensive and surprisingly nutritious. All cuts of beef, even ground, are excellent sources of iron, complete protein, zinc and niacin. Look for lean ground beef that contains no more than 17 per cent fat and be sure to drain off excess fat after browning the meat.**

# Veal Paillard with Chive Sauce

**Per Serving:**

Calories: 198

Fat: 9.7 g

Protein: 22 g

Carbohydrate: 4.9 g

Calcium: 108 mg

Iron: 1 mg

Fiber: 0.3 g

Sodium: 261 mg

Cholesterol: 81 mg

*Quick-cooking paillards are thin slices of lean meat, similar to scallopini. You can use cutlets by simply pounding them thinner between two sheets of waxed paper. Pork or turkey also works well in this recipe.*

| | | |
|---|---|---|
| 2 tsp | vegetable oil | 10 mL |
| 4 | veal cutlets (each about 3-1/2 oz/100 g) | 4 |

**Chive Sauce:**

| | | |
|---|---|---|
| 3/4 cup | chicken stock | 175 mL |
| 1/4 cup | minced shallots | 50 mL |
| 2 tbsp | finely grated peeled apple | 25 mL |
| 2 tbsp | snipped chives | 25 mL |
| 3/4 cup | low-fat yogurt | 175 mL |
| 3 tbsp | light cream cheese | 50 mL |
| | Salt and pepper | |

■ Brush 2 sheets of waxed paper with oil; place cutlets between waxed paper and pound to 1/4-inch (5 mm) thickness.

**Chive Sauce:** In small saucepan, bring chicken stock, shallots and apple to boil; reduce heat to medium, cover and cook for 5 minutes or until shallots and apple are softened. Add chives; cook over low heat for 1 minute. Whisk in yogurt, then cream cheese until smooth and heated through. Season with salt and pepper to taste.

■ Meanwhile, in hot nonstick skillet, quickly sauté veal for about 30 seconds on each side or until browned. Pool sauce on serving plate and top with veal, or spoon sauce over veal. For an attractive presentation, garnish the dish with additional chives and a tomato rose. Makes 4 servings.

**MENU SUGGESTION**

PORK TENDERLOIN SCALLOPINI
WITH PARSNIP-PEAR SAUCE
*This Page*

*STEAMED BROCCOLI*

CHUTNEY RICE SALAD
*Page 103*

YOGURT AND FRESH FRUIT PARFAIT
*Page 118*

# Pork Tenderloin Scallopini with Parsnip-Pear Sauce

**Per Serving:**

Calories: 199

Fat: 4.6 g

Protein: 26.6 g

Carbohydrate: 12.4 g

Calcium: 26 mg

Iron: 1.8 mg

Fiber: 2.3 g

Sodium: 307 mg

Cholesterol: 62 mg

*Puréed fruit and vegetable sauces have fewer calories than heavier gravies.*

| | | |
|---|---|---|
| 1 lb | pork tenderloin | 500 g |

**Marinade:**

| | | |
|---|---|---|
| 1 | clove garlic, minced | 1 |
| 1 tbsp | soy sauce | 15 mL |
| 1 tbsp | raspberry or rice wine vinegar | 15 mL |

**Parsnip-Pear Sauce:**

| | | |
|---|---|---|
| 1 | parsnip, peeled and thinly sliced | 1 |
| 1 | pear, cored, peeled and coarsely chopped | 1 |
| 1 tsp | raspberry or rice wine vinegar | 5 mL |
| 1/2 tsp | soy sauce | 2 mL |
| 1/2 tsp | prepared horseradish | 2 mL |
| 1/4 tsp | Worcestershire sauce | 1 mL |
| 1/2 cup | boiling water | 125 mL |
| | Green onion, slivered | |

■ Cut tenderloin crosswise into 12 slices, each about 1 inch (2.5 cm) thick. Between sheets of plastic wrap, pound slices gently to 3/8-inch (9 mm) thickness.

**Marinade:** In small dish, mix together garlic, soy sauce and vinegar. Brush over both sides of pork slices. Set aside for 10 minutes.

**Parsnip-Pear Sauce:** In small saucepan of boiling water, cook parsnip for about 10 minutes or until tender; drain well. In food processor or blender, purée hot parsnip, pear, vinegar, soy sauce, horseradish and Worcestershire. With machine running, gradually pour in boiling water; process for a few seconds or until smooth. Set aside.

■ Broil pork slices 4 inches (10 cm) from heat, in batches if necessary, for 2 to 3 mintues on each side or until meat is no longer pink and begins to brown. (Alternatively, grill in nonstick skillet.)

■ Spoon a few spoonfuls sauce onto each warmed dinner plate. Arrange 3 slices of pork on top. Garnish with green onion. Serve with remaining sauce. Makes 4 servings.

---

**PUMP UP YOUR IRON**

Even though we all need iron for our red blood cells *(see Daily Nutritional Guidelines on page 136 for recommended daily iron intake)*, our bodies absorb only 10 to 20 per cent of the iron we eat. And heme iron — found only in meats, poultry, fish and seafood — is absorbed better than the non-heme iron found in eggs, grains, dried beans, nuts, vegetables and fruits.

To make sure you're getting enough iron, include more of these iron-rich foods in your diet.

| Food | Iron (mg) |
|---|---|
| 3 oz (90 g) pork liver | 26.1 |
| 3 oz (90 g) beef kidney | 11.8 |
| 3 oz (90 g) beef or chicken liver | 8.0 |
| 1/2 cup (125 mL) prune juice | 5.5 |
| 9 small oysters | 5.0 |
| 1 cup (250 mL) baked beans | 4.9 |
| 3/4 cup (200 mL) whole grain cereal | 4.5 |
| 2 oz (60 g) liverwurst | 3.2 |
| 1 tbsp (15 mL) blackstrap molasses | 3.2 |
| 1/2 cup (125 mL) pitted dates, prunes or raisins | 2.5 |

# Tex-Mex Liver Stir-Fry

**Per Serving:**

Calories: 203

Fat: 10 g

Protein: 16.2 g

Carbohydrate: 13 g

Calcium: 23 mg

Iron: 4.9 mg

Fiber: 2.2 g

Sodium: 376 mg

Cholesterol: 228 mg

*Even though liver is high in cholesterol, it's also an excellent source of iron. With this delicious recipe, it's easy to serve liver more often. For our photo, we served the stir-fry in tortillas and spooned sauce over top.*

| | | |
|---|---|---|
| 3/4 lb | beef liver | 375 g |
| | Whole wheat flour | |
| 2 tbsp | vegetable oil | 25 mL |
| 1 | clove garlic, minced | 1 |
| 1 | onion | 1 |
| 1 | sweet red or green pepper | 1 |
| Pinch | cayenne pepper | Pinch |
| 1 | can (7-1/2 oz/213 mL) tomato sauce | 1 |
| 1/4 cup | water | 50 mL |
| 1 tbsp | vinegar | 15 mL |
| | Salt and pepper | |

*Tex-Mex Liver Stir-Fry*

■ Trim skin and heavy veins from liver. Cut into thin strips about 3 inches (8 cm) long. Pat dry with paper towels. Dredge in flour, shaking off excess.

■ In large nonstick skillet, heat oil and garlic over medium heat; stir-fry liver for about 4 minutes or until lightly browned. Remove to warm plate.

■ Quarter onion and red pepper; slice thinly. Add to skillet and stir-fry for 2 to 3 minutes. Stir in cayenne pepper, tomato sauce and water; cook, stirring occasionally, for about 3 minutes or until onion is tender-crisp. Stir in vinegar and liver. Season with salt and pepper to taste. Makes 4 servings.

**MENU SUGGESTION**

BLANQUETTE OF VEAL
WITH ONIONS AND MUSHROOMS
*This Page*

STEAMED NEW POTATOES

PEAS AND GREEN ONIONS
*Page 105*

ANGEL FOOD CAKE
with RASPBERRY FRUIT SAUCE
*Page 118*

# Blanquette of Veal with Onions and Mushrooms

**Per Serving:**

Calories: 254

Fat: 9.6 g

Protein: 24.6 g

Carbohydrate: 15.5 g

Calcium: 56 mg

Iron: 2.1 mg

Fiber: 2.1 g

Sodium: 354 mg

Cholesterol: 80 mg

*This easy veal dish is great for busy weekday suppers or weekend entertaining. Serve with egg noodles and a salad of mixed greens.*

| | | |
|---|---|---|
| 2 cups | pearl onions | 500 mL |
| 1 lb | lean stewing veal | 500 g |
| 2 tsp | vegetable oil | 10 mL |
| 1-1/2 cups | chicken stock | 375 mL |
| 1/2 cup | dry white wine | 125 mL |
| 2 | sprigs fresh parsley | 2 |
| 1 | bay leaf | 1 |
| 1 | clove garlic, minced | 1 |
| 1 | stalk celery, chopped | 1 |
| 1 | carrot, sliced diagonally | 1 |
| 1/2 tsp | dried thyme | 2 mL |
| 2 cups | button mushrooms | 500 mL |
| 3 tbsp | each cornstarch and water | 50 mL |
| 1/2 cup | light sour cream | 125 mL |
| 2 tbsp | finely chopped fresh dill or parsley | 25 mL |
| 1 tbsp | lemon juice | 15 mL |
| Pinch | nutmeg | Pinch |
| | Salt and pepper | |

■ Cover onions with boiling water; let stand for 2 minutes. Rinse under cold water; peel and set aside. Cut veal into 1-inch (2.5 cm) pieces; set aside.

*Blanquette of Veal with Onions and Mushrooms*

■ In large heavy saucepan or Dutch oven, heat oil over medium-high heat; cook veal, turning often, until browned. Add stock, wine, parsley sprigs, bay leaf, garlic, celery, carrot and thyme; bring to simmer. Reduce heat to medium-low and cook, covered, for 20 to 25 minutes or until veal is almost tender.

■ Add reserved onions and mushrooms; cook, covered, for 8 minutes or until veal and vegetables are tender. With slotted spoon, remove meat and vegetables to bowl. Discard parsley sprigs and bay leaf.

■ Blend cornstarch with water; whisk into pan liquid and cook, stirring, over medium-high heat until thickened and smooth. Stir in sour cream and dill. Return veal and vegetables to pan; cook over medium heat just until heated through. Stir in lemon juice, nutmeg, and salt and pepper to taste. Makes 4 servings.

**GIVE YOUR FAVORITE RECIPE A HEALTHY MAKEOVER**
Streamline your favorite family recipes to meet today's faster and healthier style of cooking.
■ Reduce the amount of fat and sugar. When you need some fat, use a polyunsaturated or monounsaturated vegetable oil instead of butter, shortening or bacon fat.
■ Increase the fiber in salads, soups and stews by adding cooked legumes like chickpeas or lentils.
■ Flavor dishes with spices and herbs instead of salt.
■ Cut down on portion sizes.
■ Retain the nutrients, color and texture of vegetables by shortening the cooking time or using the microwave oven.

## Grilled Pork Tenderloin with Spicy Plum Sauce

**Per Serving:**

Calories: 294

Fat: 9.3 g

Protein: 26.5 g

Carbohydrate: 26.1 g

Calcium: 29 mg

Iron: 2 mg

Fiber: 1.4 g

Sodium: 65 mg

Cholesterol: 62 mg

*A generous basting of spicy plum sauce adds flavor and color to grilled tenderloin.*

| | | |
|---|---|---|
| 2 | pork tenderloins (each 3/4 lb/375 g) | 2 |
| 1 tbsp | vegetable oil | 15 mL |
| | Salt and pepper | |

**Spicy Plum Sauce:**

| | | |
|---|---|---|
| 1 tbsp | vegetable oil | 15 mL |
| Half | onion, finely chopped | Half |
| 1/4 tsp | each ground allspice, ginger, cloves and cinnamon | 1 mL |
| 3 cups | coarsely chopped purple plums (about 1 lb/500 g) | 750 mL |
| 1/2 cup | packed brown sugar | 125 mL |
| 1/3 cup | orange juice | 75 mL |
| 1 tsp | grated orange rind | 5 mL |

**Spicy Plum Sauce:** In large saucepan, heat oil over medium heat; cook onion for 2 minutes or until softened. Stir in allspice, ginger, cloves and cinnamon; cook, stirring, for 1 minute.

■ Add plums, sugar, orange juice, and rind; bring to boil and cook over medium heat for 15 minutes or until thickened. Purée in food processor. Reserve 1 cup (250 mL) to serve with pork.

■ Trim excess fat from pork. Brush with oil and sprinkle lightly with salt and pepper. Tuck ends under and tie tenderloins with string soaked in water. On greased grill 4 to 6 inches (10 to 15 cm) from medium-hot coals, cook pork, covered, for 10 minutes. Turn meat over and cook for 10 minutes longer. Brush with plum sauce and cook, turning and brushing with sauce, for about 10 minutes or until pork is no longer pink inside (170°F/75°C on meat thermometer). Slice and serve with reserved plum sauce. Makes 6 servings.

*Grilled Pork Tenderloin with Spicy Plum Sauce*

MENU SUGGESTION

LAMB PILAF
*This Page*

CUCUMBER AND YOGURT SALAD

FRESH FRUIT

# Lamb Pilaf

**Per Serving:**

Calories: 365

Fat: 10 g

Protein: 29.9 g

Carbohydrate: 38.9 g

Calcium: 101 mg

Iron: 3.9 mg

Fiber: 5.1 g

Sodium: 837 mg

Cholesterol: 84 mg

*Brown rice is used instead of white rice in this recipe because it has more fiber and B vitamins as well as a wonderful nutty taste.*

| | | |
|---|---|---|
| 1 | large clove garlic, finely chopped | 1 |
| 2 | onions, finely chopped | 2 |
| 2 | carrots, thinly sliced | 2 |
| 1 cup | sliced mushrooms | 250 mL |
| 2 cups | tomato juice | 500 mL |
| 1 tsp | crumbled dried rosemary | 5 mL |
| 2 cups | cooked brown rice | 500 mL |
| 1 cup | frozen peas | 250 mL |
| 1 lb | lean boneless lamb loin | 500 g |
| 2 tsp | olive oil | 10 mL |
| 2 tbsp | freshly grated Parmesan cheese | 25 mL |
| | Salt and pepper | |

■ In heavy saucepan, combine garlic, onion, carrots and mushrooms. Add tomato juice, rosemary and rice; bring to boil. Reduce heat to medium and cook, stirring occasionally, for about 5 minutes or until onion is tender, adding a little water if moisture evaporates too quickly. Add peas and cook for 2 minutes; cover and keep warm.

■ Meanwhile, slice lamb thinly into bite-size strips. In skillet, heat oil over medium-high heat; stir-fry lamb for about 3 minutes or just until no longer pink. Add rice mixture and stir to scrape up any brown bits. Stir in Parmesan. Season with salt and pepper to taste. Cook just until heated through. Makes 4 servings.

# Pork Stir-Fry

*Use any lean cut of pork, trimmed of visible fat, in this quick and easy stir-fry. Serve with rice or oriental noodles.*

| | | |
|---|---|---|
| 1/3 cup | chicken stock | 75 mL |
| 2 tbsp | oyster sauce | 25 mL |
| 1-1/2 tsp | cornstarch | 7 mL |
| 1/2 tsp | sesame oil | 2 mL |
| Dash | hot pepper sauce | Dash |
| 1 tbsp | vegetable oil | 15 mL |
| 3/4 lb | lean pork, trimmed and thinly sliced | 375 g |
| 1 tbsp | minced gingerroot | 15 mL |
| 2 | cloves garlic, minced | 2 |
| 2 | carrots, sliced diagonally | 2 |
| 2 | stalks celery, sliced diagonally | 2 |
| 2 cups | snow peas, trimmed | 500 mL |
| 1 cup | bean sprouts | 250 mL |
| 2 tbsp | chopped cashews (optional) | 25 mL |

**Per Serving:**

Calories: 217

Fat: 7.8 g

Protein: 23.1 g

Carbohydrate: 13.5 g

Calcium: 57 mg

Iron: 2.9 mg

Fiber: 4.8 g

Sodium: 154 mg

Cholesterol: 46 mg

■ Combine chicken stock, oyster sauce, cornstarch, sesame oil and hot pepper sauce; set aside.

■ In large nonstick skillet, heat oil over medium-high heat for 1 minute or until very hot. Stir-fry pork, ginger and garlic for 1 minute or until pork is no longer pink. Add carrots, celery and snow peas; stir-fry for 1 minute. Stir in chicken stock mixture; cook, stirring, for 1 minute. Reduce heat to medium; cover and steam for 1-1/2 minutes or until vegetables are tender-crisp. Stir in bean sprouts; cook, uncovered, for 1 minute. Transfer to serving dish; garnish with cashews (if using). Makes 4 servings.

# Chunky Pork Stew

**Per Serving:**

Calories: 357

Fat: 10.1 g

Protein: 30.3 g

Carbohydrate: 35.9 g

Calcium: 75 mg

Iron: 3.1 mg

Fiber: 6 g

Sodium: 387 mg

Cholesterol: 54 mg

*In this lean version of an old favorite, we increased the vegetables and reduced the amount of meat for 4 servings. If using new potatoes, leave the skins on for extra fiber.*

| 1 lb | lean pork, cut in 1-inch (2.5 cm) cubes | 500 g |
|---|---|---|
| 2 tbsp | all-purpose flour | 25 mL |
| 1 tbsp | vegetable oil | 15 mL |
| 5 | onions | 5 |
| 1 | clove garlic, minced | 1 |
| 2 | carrots, sliced | 2 |
| 1 | stalk celery, sliced | 1 |
| 1-1/2 tsp | chopped fresh thyme (or 1/2 tsp/2 mL dried) | 7 mL |
| 1/4 tsp | pepper | 1 mL |
| 1-1/3 cups | chicken stock | 325 mL |
| 2 | potatoes, quartered | 2 |
| 1 cup | frozen peas | 250 mL |
| 1 tbsp | cold water | 15 mL |

■ Lightly dust pork with about half of the flour. In heavy ovenproof skillet, heat 2 tsp (10 mL) of the oil over medium-high heat; brown pork. Remove and set aside.

■ Chop 1 of the onions; add remaining oil, chopped onion, garlic, carrots, celery, thyme and pepper to skillet; reduce heat to medium-low, cover and cook for about 5 minutes or until vegetables are softened and browned. Add chicken stock, stirring to scrape up brown bits from bottom of skillet.

■ Return pork to skillet; cover and bake in 350°F (180°C) oven for 20 minutes. Add potatoes and remaining whole onions; bake for 20 minutes. Add peas. Stir remaining flour into water; stir into skillet. Bake for 10 minutes or until stew boils and thickens. Adjust seasoning, adding salt if desired. Makes 4 servings.

*Chunky Pork Stew*

## Oriental Lamb Chops with Vegetables

**Per Serving:**

Calories: 260

Fat: 17.7 g

Protein: 16.7 g

Carbohydrate: 8.3 g

Calcium: 40 mg

Iron: 2.2 mg

Fiber: 1.8 g

Sodium: 869 mg

Cholesterol: 71 mg

*For even cooking, make sure the vegetables are no thicker than the lamb chops.*

| 8 | lamb loin chops (1 inch/2.5 cm thick) | 8 |
|---|---|---|
| 1/4 cup | soy sauce | 50 mL |
| 2 tbsp | mirin (rice wine for cooking) or dry sherry | 25 mL |
| 2 | cloves garlic, minced | 2 |
| 1 tbsp | minced gingerroot | 15 mL |
| 2 tsp | sesame oil | 10 mL |
| 1/2 tsp | Chinese five-spice powder* | 2 mL |
| 1/4 tsp | pepper | 1 mL |
| 4 | small onions, parboiled | 4 |
| 1 | tomato, cut in eighths | 1 |
| 1 | sweet green pepper, cut in chunks | 1 |

■ Trim excess fat from lamb; slash remaining fat at edges to prevent curling. Arrange in single layer in plastic bag set in shallow dish.

■ Stir together soy sauce, mirin, garlic, gingerroot, sesame oil, five-spice powder and pepper; pour over chops and turn to coat well. Tie bag closed and marinate at room temperature for 30 minutes, turning occasionally. (Alternatively, marinate in refrigerator overnight; let stand at room temperature for 30 minutes before grilling.)

■ Remove chops from marinade, reserving marinade. Pat chops dry with paper towels. On each of 4 greased metal skewers, thread 2 chops lengthwise, along with onions, tomatoes and green pepper, making sure that chops can lie flat on grill.

■ On greased grill 4 inches (10 cm) from hot coals or at high setting, cook chops, brushing occasionally with marinade, for 4 minutes. Turn chops over and cook for 3 to 4 minutes longer for rare or until desired doneness. Makes 4 servings.

*Available at Chinese grocery stores.

## Pork Slices with Mustard Applesauce

*This recipe can easily be doubled. For a lively flavor variation, try 1/2 tsp (2 mL) curry powder instead of mustard.*

| 1 | pork tenderloin (about 3/4 lb/375 g) | 1 |
|---|---|---|
| 1 tbsp | hoisin sauce | 15 mL |
| 1/2 cup | applesauce | 125 mL |
| 1 tsp | chopped fresh parsley | 5 mL |
| 1-1/2 tsp | Dijon mustard | 7 mL |

■ Place pork tenderloin on rack in baking dish with small end tucked under. Brush with hoisin sauce. Roast in 400°F (200°C) oven for 40 minutes or until meat thermometer registers 160 to 170°F (71 to 75°C) and meat is no longer pink inside.

■ Meanwhile, blend applesauce, parsley and mustard to make dipping sauce. Cut tenderloin into 1/2-inch (1 cm) thick slices; serve warm or at room temperature with dipping sauce. Makes 4 servings.

**Per Serving:**

Calories: 147

Fat: 3.6 g

Protein: 19.8 g

Carbohydrate: 8 g

Calcium: 10 mg

Iron: 1.2 mg

Fiber: 0.6 g

Sodium: 156 mg

Cholesterol: 46 mg

### LEAN TOWARD MEAT

■ In beef, look for sirloin tip, eye of round, round steak, flank steak, lean stew meat, tenderloin, or lean ground beef.

■ The leanest cuts of lamb are the leg and sirloin chop.

■ Veal is naturally lean, except for the breast.

■ The leanest cut of pork is the tenderloin, then leg cuts like schnitzel or pork leg roast.

■ Trim all visible fat from meat.

■ Roast, bake, broil or barbecue meats whenever possible. If you have to fry, use a nonstick pan and a small amount of vegetable oil, and drain off fat after browning.

## Sirloin with Balsamic Vinegar

**Per Serving:**

Calories: 283

Fat: 17.1 g

Protein: 27.8 g

Carbohydrate: 1.7 g

Calcium: 31 mg

Iron: 3.4 mg

Fiber: 0.1 g

Sodium: 79 mg

Cholesterol: 70 mg

*Sirloin is one of the most flavorful and tender cuts of beef but you can also use flank steak. (You'll need 2, each approx. 1 to 1-1/2 lb/500 to 750 g, and be sure to marinate overnight.) If you can't find balsamic vinegar, substitute a good red wine vinegar.*

| | | |
|---|---|---|
| 3 lb | sirloin steak (2 in/5 cm thick) | 1.5 kg |
| 2 tbsp | olive oil | 25 mL |
| | Salt | |

**Marinade:**

| | | |
|---|---|---|
| 1 cup | dry Italian red wine | 250 mL |
| 3 tbsp | extra-virgin olive oil | 50 mL |
| 3 tbsp | balsamic vinegar | 50 mL |
| 2 tbsp | lemon juice | 25 mL |
| 1 tbsp | Dijon mustard | 15 mL |
| 2 | cloves garlic, minced | 2 |
| 1 tsp | each dried rosemary and thyme | 5 mL |
| 1 tsp | pepper | 5 mL |
| 1/2 tsp | dried oregano | 2 mL |

**Marinade:** In large shallow dish, combine wine, oil, vinegar, lemon juice, mustard, garlic, rosemary, thyme, pepper and oregano. Pat steak dry and add to dish, turning to coat. Cover and marinate for 1 to 2 hours in refrigerator.

■ Remove steak and pat dry; pour marinade into saucepan and set aside. Brush steak with oil if needed. Broil or barbecue about 5 inches (12 cm) from heat for 7 to 10 minutes per side for rare or until desired doneness. Let stand for 5 minutes before carving diagonally across the grain into thin slices.

■ Meanwhile, bring marinade to boil; boil, uncovered, for 8 minutes or until thickened and reduced to about 1/2 cup (125 mL). Taste and season with salt if necessary. Serve a little sauce with each portion of meat. Makes 8 servings.

**MENU SUGGESTION**

SIRLOIN WITH BALSAMIC VINEGAR
*This Page*

STEAMED GREEN BEANS
and
CARROT MEDALLIONS

POACHED PEARS IN CRANBERRY JUICE
*Page 117*

## Scallopini with Oriental Orange Sauce

*Very thin 1/4-inch (5 mm) slices can be cut from the tenderloin, loin or leg of lamb to make lamb scallopini. This recipe can also be prepared with beef or chicken.*

**Per Serving:**

Calories: 345

Fat: 14.6 g

Protein: 33.4 g

Carbohydrate: 18 g

Calcium: 26 mg

Iron: 3.3 mg

Fiber: 0.7 g

Sodium: 578 mg

Cholesterol: 107 mg

| | | |
|---|---|---|
| 1/2 cup | all-purpose flour | 125 mL |
| | Salt and pepper | |
| 1-1/2 lb | lamb scallopini | 750 g |
| 2 tbsp | (approx) peanut oil | 25 mL |
| 1 | clove garlic, finely chopped | 1 |
| 1 tsp | finely chopped gingerroot | 5 mL |
| 2 | green onions, chopped | 2 |
| 1/3 cup | water | 75 mL |
| 2 tbsp | unsweetened frozen orange juice concentrate | 25 mL |
| 2 tbsp | soy sauce | 25 mL |
| 1 tbsp | hoisin sauce | 15 mL |

■ In shallow dish, season flour with salt and pepper to taste. Pat meat dry; dredge with flour mixture.

■ In large skillet, heat oil over medium-high heat; cook meat, in batches and adding more oil if necessary, for about 2 minutes per side or just until cooked through. Remove to platter and keep warm.

■ Add garlic, gingerroot and green onions to skillet; cook for 1 minute. Pour in water, orange juice concentrate, soy sauce and hoisin sauce; bring to boil, stirring constantly. Pour over meat. Makes 4 servings.

*Sirloin with Balsamic Vinegar*

## Broccoli-Stuffed Turkey Loaf

**Per Serving:**

Calories: 189

Fat: 4 g

Protein: 22.3 g

Carbohydrate: 15.9 g

Calcium: 114 mg

Iron: 2.7 mg

Fiber: 2.3 g

Sodium: 540 mg

Cholesterol: 48 mg

*Ground turkey is now available in many supermarkets. If you can't find it, ask the butcher to grind some.*

| | | |
|---|---|---|
| 2-1/2 cups | chopped broccoli (about 1 bunch) | 625 mL |
| 1-1/2 lb | ground turkey | 750 g |
| 1 cup | fine fresh bread crumbs | 250 mL |
| 1 tsp | salt | 5 mL |
| 1/2 tsp | dried marjoram | 2 mL |
| 1/4 tsp | pepper | 1 mL |
| Pinch | dried thyme | Pinch |

**Tomato Sauce:**

| | | |
|---|---|---|
| 1/4 cup | water | 50 mL |
| 1 | onion, chopped | 1 |
| 1 | clove garlic, minced | 1 |
| 1 | can (19 oz/540 mL) tomatoes (undrained) | 1 |
| 2 tbsp | chopped fresh parsley | 25 mL |
| | Salt and pepper | |

**Tomato Sauce:** In saucepan, heat water over medium heat. Add onion and garlic; simmer, stirring often, for 5 to 7 minutes or until onion is tender. Remove 1 tbsp (15 mL) onion-garlic mixture and set aside. Add tomatoes, breaking up with fork; bring to boil. Reduce heat and simmer for 20 minutes or until thickened. Stir in parsley; season with salt and pepper to taste.

■ In saucepan of boiling water, cook broccoli for 2 minutes or until tender-crisp. Drain and refresh under cold water; drain again and pat dry. Set aside.

■ Combine turkey, reserved onion-garlic mixture, bread crumbs, salt, marjoram, pepper and thyme; mix thoroughly. Place on waxed paper; pat into rectangle about 15 × 8 inches (38 × 20 cm). Sprinkle with broccoli, leaving 1/2-inch (1 cm) border. Roll up turkey mixture from short end, jelly-roll style, lifting with paper. Place, seam side down, on greased baking sheet. Bake in 350°F (180°C) oven for 1 hour or until browned and juices run clear.

■ To serve, spoon half of the Tomato Sauce over turkey loaf; pass remaining sauce. Makes 8 servings.

## Grilled Lemon and Rosemary Chicken

*Because you can remove the visible fat from skinless chicken, it's healthier for you than when cooked with the skin on. But skinless chicken often dries out during grilling. By soaking it in buttermilk or low-fat yogurt, you add moisture and a tangy flavor.*

**Per Serving:**

Calories: 246

Fat: 9.3 g

Protein: 36.4 g

Carbohydrate: 2.3 g

Calcium: 43 mg

Iron: 1.5 mg

Fiber: 0 g

Sodium: 127 mg

Cholesterol: 110 mg

| | | |
|---|---|---|
| 2 cups | buttermilk or low-fat yogurt | 500 mL |
| 1/4 cup | lemon juice | 50 mL |
| 4 | chicken quarters (2-1/2 lb/1.25 kg total) | 4 |
| | Fresh rosemary sprigs | |
| | Lemon slices | |

■ In heavy plastic bag, combine buttermilk and lemon juice; add chicken and a few rosemary sprigs. Close bag, pressing out as much air as possible. Refrigerate for at least 2 or up to 8 hours, turning bag occasionally.

■ Remove chicken from buttermilk mixture, scraping off excess. Place on greased grill over medium-hot coals or at medium-high setting; cover and cook for 15 minutes.

■ Turn chicken over; top each piece with 2 or 3 lemon slices and rosemary sprigs. Cook for 15 to 20 minutes longer or until juices run clear when chicken is pierced. Serve garnished with more lemon and rosemary. Makes 4 servings.

# Quick Chicken Curry

**Per Serving:**

Calories: 225

Fat: 4.6 g

Protein: 28.6 g

Carbohydrate: 17.2 g

Calcium: 37 mg

Iron: 2.1 mg

Fiber: 2.8 g

Sodium: 159 mg

Cholesterol: 71 mg

*Serve this curry over rice or noodles and offer chutney or plain yogurt as an accompaniment.*

| | | |
|---|---|---|
| 1 tsp | vegetable oil | 5 mL |
| 1 | onion, chopped | 1 |
| 1 lb | boneless skinless chicken breasts, cubed | 500 g |
| 1 tbsp | curry powder | 15 mL |
| 2 tsp | all-purpose flour | 10 mL |
| 3/4 cup | chicken stock | 175 mL |
| 1/4 cup | slivered dried apricots or raisins | 50 mL |
| 1/4 tsp | ginger | 1 mL |
| 1 | pear (unpeeled), cubed | 1 |
| | Salt and pepper | |

■ In nonstick saucepan, heat oil over medium heat for 1 minute; add onion, stirring to coat. Reduce heat to medium-low; cover and cook for 5 minutes or until onion is softened and almost translucent, stirring occasionally.

■ Add chicken and cook, stirring, until no longer pink outside. Add curry powder and cook, stirring, for 30 seconds. Blend flour into stock until smooth. Add to pan along with apricots and ginger; cook, stirring, until liquid thickens. Cover and cook over medium-low heat, stirring occasionally, for 5 minutes or until chicken is no longer pink inside.

■ Add pear; cover and cook for 2 minutes or until just tender and heated through. Makes 4 servings.

*Broccoli-Stuffed Turkey Loaf*

# Chicken and Pink Grapefruit

**Per Serving:**

Calories: 292

Fat: 7.7 g

Protein: 30.1 g

Carbohydrate: 24.7 g

Calcium: 37 mg

Iron: 1.5 mg

Fiber: 0.4 g

Sodium: 89 mg

Cholesterol: 91 mg

*If you remove the skin from the chicken to cut down on fat, bake in a covered casserole or baking dish to keep the chicken juicy.*

| 2 lb | chicken pieces | 1 kg |
|------|----------------|------|
| 1 cup | grapefruit juice | 250 mL |
| 1/2 tsp | grated grapefruit rind | 2 mL |
| 2 tbsp | maple syrup or liquid honey | 25 mL |
| 2 tbsp | finely chopped preserved or crystallized ginger | 25 mL |
| 1 tbsp | cornstarch | 15 mL |
| 1 | pink or red grapefruit, peeled and sectioned | 1 |

■ Arrange chicken skin side up in single layer in shallow casserole or baking dish. Bake, uncovered, in 375°F (190°C) oven for 30 minutes. Drain off accumulated liquid.

■ Meanwhile, in saucepan, mix together grapefruit juice and rind, maple syrup, ginger and cornstarch; bring to boil, stirring constantly. Reduce heat and cook for about 1 minute or until sauce is smooth and thickened slightly. Pour evenly over chicken and bake, uncovered and basting occasionally, for about 25 minutes or until chicken is no longer pink inside. Add grapefruit and bake for about 5 minutes longer or until warm. Makes 4 servings.

*Chicken and Pink Grapefruit*

---

**A TOAST TO GOOD HEALTH**

Cold, wet, wonderful water! Your body can't get along without it — and neither can you. Get into the habit of drinking a glass of water before every meal. It's an easy way to start feeling full even before you sit down to eat. And make sure you have water after you exercise, especially if you've worked up a good sweat.

Contrary to popular belief, liquids like fruit juices and even tea and coffee count as part of your daily water intake.

# Chicken Vegetable Stir-Fry

**Per Serving:**

Calories: 327

Fat: 12.6 g

Protein: 30.3 g

Carbohydrate: 24.3 g

Calcium: 130 mg

Iron: 3 mg

Fiber: 3.9 g

Sodium: 432 mg

Cholesterol: 70 mg

*Keep track of fat by measuring it carefully: you can make a little go a long way in stir-fry cooking by using a good-quality nonstick skillet. This recipe can easily be doubled to serve 4.*

| | | |
|---|---|---|
| 1/2 lb | boneless skinless chicken breasts | 250 g |
| 1 tsp | lemon juice | 5 mL |
| 1 tbsp | cornstarch | 15 mL |
| Pinch | pepper | Pinch |
| 1/2 cup | apple juice | 125 mL |
| 2 tbsp | chicken stock | 25 mL |
| 2 tsp | soy sauce | 10 mL |
| 1/2 tsp | Worcestershire sauce | 2 mL |
| 1 | small onion | 1 |
| Half | sweet green pepper | Half |
| 1 | carrot | 1 |
| 1 | small stalk broccoli | 1 |
| 4 tsp | vegetable oil | 20 mL |
| 1 cup | bean sprouts | 250 mL |

■ Cut chicken crosswise into 1-inch (2.5 cm) wide strips. In small bowl, toss chicken with lemon juice, 2 tsp (10 mL) of the cornstarch and pepper; set aside. Blend remaining cornstarch, apple juice, chicken stock, soy sauce and Worcestershire sauce; set aside.

■ Quarter onion lengthwise and separate layers. Cut green pepper into 1/2-inch (1 cm) wide strips. Thinly slice carrot diagonally. Break broccoli florets into small pieces; peel stem and cut diagonally into 1/4-inch (5 mm) slices.

■ In nonstick skillet, heat half of the oil over medium-high heat; stir-fry chicken for 5 minutes or until no longer pink inside. Transfer to plate.

■ Add remaining oil to skillet. Add onion, green pepper, carrot and broccoli; stir-fry for 1 minute or just until broccoli brightens in color. Add apple juice mixture; cook, stirring constantly, until thickened, about 2 minutes. Return chicken to pan. Reduce heat to medium, cover and cook for 2 minutes or until vegetables are tender-crisp. Stir in bean sprouts and heat through. Taste and adjust seasoning if necessary. Makes 2 servings.

## CHICKEN KNOW-HOW

■ **Store chicken in the coldest part of the refrigerator for up to 48 hours, or in the freezer for up to six months.**

■ **Serve cooked chicken on a clean platter — never on one that's held raw chicken or other meats.**

■ **Refrigerate cooked chicken immediately without waiting for it to cool.**

■ **Use a polyethylene chopping surface, not wood, for cutting poultry. Immediately after using, wash surface and utensils in hot soapy water with a few drops of chlorine bleach. Rinse well and dry.**

■ **Cook meat until meat thermometer registers 185°F (85°C). When cooked, the white meat should show no trace of pink, and juices of dark meat should run clear when pierced with a fork.**

■ **To cut calories and fat, remove the skin from chicken either before cooking or after.**

## Turkey Paillards with Yogurt-Mango Salsa

**Per Serving:**

Calories: 283

Fat: 5.5 g

Protein: 43.5 g

Carbohydrate: 13.4 g

Calcium: 138 mg

Iron: 2.3 mg

Fiber: 1.2 g

Sodium: 274 mg

Cholesterol: 114 mg

*Turkey paillards, cutlets and scallopini are fast becoming popular alternatives to veal. Sliced diagonally off the breast, the paillard is usually about 1/4 inch (5 mm) thick. The salsa's refreshing contrast of cool yogurt and tangy chili complements turkey perfectly. Serve the dish with rice mixed with pine nuts.*

| | | |
|---|---|---|
| 1-1/2 lb | turkey paillards | 750 g |
| 1 tbsp | vegetable oil | 15 mL |
| | Salt and pepper | |

**Yogurt-Mango Salsa:**

| | | |
|---|---|---|
| 1 cup | low-fat yogurt | 250 mL |
| 3 tbsp | chopped canned chilies | 50 mL |
| 1 | mango, peeled and diced | 1 |
| 3 tbsp | chopped fresh mint | 50 mL |
| 3 tbsp | chopped chives or green onions | 50 mL |
| 1/4 tsp | salt | 1 mL |
| 1/4 tsp | hot pepper sauce | 1 mL |

**Yogurt-Mango Salsa:** Combine yogurt, chilies, mango, mint, chives, salt and hot pepper sauce; taste and adjust seasoning if necessary.
■ Brush turkey with oil; season with salt and pepper to taste.
■ To broil or barbecue, brush hot broiler pan or grill with oil; heat for 2 minutes. Cook paillards for 2 to 3 minutes per side or just until cooked through. Serve hot or cold with salsa. Makes 4 servings.

### PAILLARDS AND SCALLOPINI

With today's trend toward light and quick meals, thin lean cuts of meat are more popular than ever. The names paillard and scallopini refer to thinly cut boneless slices of meat that have no fat or gristle. The thinness makes the meat extremely tender and the preparation very fast.

**MENU SUGGESTION**

TURKEY PAILLARDS
WITH YOGURT-MANGO SALSA
*This Page*

BROWN RICE

LIGHT COLESLAW
*Page 102*

CRUNCHY SEED COOKIES
*Page 135*

## Glazed Chicken Breasts

*Fast, easy and trimmed of excess fat, this chicken is wonderful served with pasta or new potatoes and grilled Spanish and red onions — as we did for our cover photograph. A simple salad of dark and light greens, fresh herbs and a light vinaigrette rounds out the meal.*

**Per Serving:**

Calories: 238

Fat: 9.4 g

Protein: 27 g

Carbohydrate: 10.6 g

Calcium: 20 mg

Iron: 1.1 mg

Fiber: 0.3 g

Sodium: 98 mg

Cholesterol: 73 mg

| | | |
|---|---|---|
| 4 | boneless skinless chicken breasts | 4 |
| | All-purpose flour | |
| 1 tbsp | vegetable oil | 15 mL |
| 1 tbsp | margarine or butter | 15 mL |
| 2 tbsp | liquid honey | 25 mL |
| 1 tbsp | grated lemon rind | 15 mL |
| 1 tbsp | chopped fresh oregano | 15 mL |
| | White pepper | |

■ Dust chicken breasts lightly with flour. In heavy nonstick skillet, heat oil and margarine or butter over medium-high heat; sauté chicken for about 5 minutes or until lightly browned on both sides. Remove to baking dish; bake in 350°F (180°C) oven for 10 to 15 minutes or until chicken is no longer pink in center. (Time varies with thickness and shape of chicken.)
■ Wipe excess fat from skillet; add honey, lemon rind and oregano; cook over medium heat until bubbly. Add baked chicken breasts, turning to caramelize and coat pieces. Season with pepper to taste. Makes 4 servings.

## Chicken Stir-Fry with Spaghettini

**Per Serving:**

Calories: 558

Fat: 11 g

Protein: 33.1 g

Carbohydrate: 78.3 g

Calcium: 83 mg

Iron: 3.9 mg

Fiber: 7.3 g

Sodium: 112 mg

Cholesterol: 53 mg

*Spaghettini provides a contrasting texture to this colorful main course.*

| | | |
|---|---|---|
| 3 | boneless skinless chicken breasts (about 3/4 lb/375 g) | 3 |
| 2 tbsp | (approx) vegetable oil | 25 mL |
| 2 | large carrots, julienned | 2 |
| 1 | small onion, chopped | 1 |
| 2 tbsp | minced gingerroot | 25 mL |
| 1 cup | sliced mushrooms | 250 mL |
| 2 | cloves garlic, minced | 2 |
| 2 cups | snow peas, trimmed | 500 mL |
| 2 tbsp | dry sherry | 25 mL |
| 3 tbsp | oyster sauce | 50 mL |
| 1/2 tsp | sesame oil | 2 mL |
| Pinch | hot pepper flakes | Pinch |
| 3/4 lb | spaghettini | 375 g |
| | Chopped fresh coriander (optional) | |

■ Slice chicken into strips 1-1/2 inches (4 cm) long and 1/2 inch (1 cm) wide. In skillet or wok, heat oil over high heat; sauté chicken, stirring occasionally, for 2 minutes or until browned. Transfer chicken to plate and set aside.

■ Add carrots, onion and ginger to skillet; stir-fry, adding more oil if necessary, for 3 minutes. Add mushrooms and garlic; stir-fry for 1 minute.

■ Return chicken to skillet along with snow peas and sherry; cover and cook for 3 to 4 minutes or until chicken is no longer pink inside. Combine oyster sauce, sesame oil and hot pepper flakes; stir into skillet.

■ Meanwhile, in large pot of boiling water, cook spaghettini until tender but firm; drain well and arrange on warmed plates. Top with chicken mixture; garnish with coriander (if using). Makes 4 servings.

*Chicken Stir-Fry with Spaghettini*

*Apricot-Prune Chicken*

# Apricot-Prune Chicken

**Per Serving:**

Calories: 413

Fat: 18.8 g

Protein: 31.2 g

Carbohydrate: 31.2 g

Calcium: 62 mg

Iron: 3.9 mg

Fiber: 3.9 g

Sodium: 492 mg

Cholesterol: 102 mg

*Team this sweetly spiced chicken dish with couscous, a Moroccan grain available in many supermarkets or health food stores. Reduce fat even more by using boneless skinless chicken breasts in place of legs.*

| | | |
|---|---|---|
| 1 tbsp | vegetable oil | 15 mL |
| 8 | chicken legs (4 lb/2 kg) | 8 |
| 2 cups | chopped onions | 500 mL |
| 2 | cloves garlic, slivered | 2 |
| 1 tbsp | cumin | 15 mL |
| 2 tsp | cinnamon | 10 mL |
| 1 tsp | each turmeric and ginger | 5 mL |
| 3/4 tsp | salt | 4 mL |
| 1/2 tsp | paprika | 2 mL |
| 1-3/4 cups | chicken stock | 425 mL |
| 1/2 tsp | hot pepper sauce | 2 mL |
| 1-1/2 cups | dried pitted prunes | 375 mL |
| 3/4 cup | dried apricots | 175 mL |
| 1 tbsp | cornstarch | 15 mL |
| 2 tbsp | lemon juice | 25 mL |

■ In large heavy skillet, heat oil over high heat; cook chicken, in batches, for 10 minutes or until well browned on all sides. Remove from skillet and set aside.

■ Drain off all but 2 tbsp (25 mL) fat from skillet; cook onions, garlic, cumin, cinnamon, turmeric, ginger, salt and paprika over medium heat, stirring constantly, for 5 minutes.

■ Stir in stock and hot pepper sauce. Add chicken, prunes and apricots; bring to boil. Cover and reduce heat to low; simmer for 20 to 25 minutes or until juices run clear when chicken is pierced with fork. With slotted spoon, transfer chicken and fruit to warm platter and keep warm.

■ Blend cornstarch into 2 tbsp (25 mL) cold water. Stir into pan juices and cook until glossy and thickened, about 2 minutes. Add lemon juice. Adjust seasoning if necessary. Spoon over chicken and fruit. Makes 8 servings.

*Apricot-Prune Chicken*

**MENU SUGGESTION**

APRICOT-PRUNE CHICKEN
*Page 66*

TABOULI
*Page 86*

BAKED BANANAS
WITH RUM AND LEMON
*Page 117*

# Chicken with Peppers

*For a quick supper, nothing beats a colorful combination of meat and saucy vegetables in one dish. Serve over rice, or toss with pasta and add a generous shake of Parmesan cheese.*

| | | |
|---|---|---|
| 4 | boneless skinless chicken breasts | 4 |
| 2 tsp | vegetable oil | 10 mL |
| 1 | sweet yellow or red pepper, chopped | 1 |
| 1 | onion, chopped | 1 |
| 2 | cloves garlic, minced | 2 |
| Pinch | hot pepper flakes | Pinch |
| 2 cups | chopped peeled tomatoes | 500 mL |
| | Salt and pepper | |
| 1/3 cup | chopped fresh basil or parsley | 75 mL |
| 1/4 cup | slivered black olives (optional) | 50 mL |

**Per Serving:**

Calories: 195

Fat: 5.7 g

Protein: 28.1 g

Carbohydrate: 7.3 g

Calcium: 36 mg

Iron: 2 mg

Fiber: 2.1 g

Sodium: 76 mg

Cholesterol: 72 mg

■ Cut chicken into bite-size pieces. In large skillet, heat oil over high heat; sauté chicken for about 3 minutes or until light golden. Remove with slotted spoon and set aside; pour off all but about 1 tsp (5 mL) fat.

■ Reduce heat to medium and cook yellow pepper, onion, garlic and hot pepper flakes for about 5 minutes or until softened. Stir in tomatoes; bring to boil, stirring occasionally. Cook, stirring, for about 5 minutes or until thickened.

■ Return chicken to skillet and season with salt and pepper to taste; cook for about 2 minutes or until chicken is no longer pink inside. Stir in basil, and olives (if using). Makes 4 servings.

**Stir-frying is one of the easiest ways to prepare a tasty and nutritious meal. Stir-fry dishes combine a small amount of meat with a generous selection of vegetables, all cooked in a minimum amount of oil. Remember to use a nonstick skillet or wok. Because the meat and vegetables cook so quickly, they retain their color, texture, flavor — *and* nutrients!**

# Ginger Chicken Stir-Fry

**Per Serving:**

Calories: 189

Fat: 9.2 g

Protein: 19.5 g

Carbohydrate: 6.7 g

Calcium: 27 mg

Iron: 1.3 mg

Fiber: 1.4 g

Sodium: 261 mg

Cholesterol: 50 mg

*Serve this tasty stir-fry with rice for a quick and easy supper.*

| | | |
|---|---|---|
| 1 tbsp | vegetable oil | 15 mL |
| 2 tbsp | slivered gingerroot | 25 mL |
| 1 | clove garlic, minced | 1 |
| 2 | boneless skinless chicken breasts, cubed | 2 |
| 2 | onions, chopped | 2 |
| 1 | sweet red or green pepper, diced | 1 |
| 1 cup | sliced mushrooms | 250 mL |
| 1 tbsp | soy sauce | 15 mL |
| 1 tbsp | oyster sauce | 15 mL |
| 2 tbsp | chopped fresh coriander, mint or green onion | 25 mL |

■ In skillet or wok, heat oil over high heat; stir-fry ginger and garlic for 30 seconds or until fragrant.

■ Add chicken; stir-fry for 2 to 4 minutes or until lightly browned. Add onions, sweet pepper and mushrooms; stir-fry for 1 to 3 minutes or until softened. Stir in soy and oyster sauces, tossing to coat. Sprinkle with coriander. Makes 4 servings.

**MENU SUGGESTION**

GRILLED WHITEFISH
*This Page*

GREEN BEAN AND RED PEPPER SALAD
*Page 106*

BREAD STICKS

WATERMELON SHERBET
*Page 129*

# Grilled Whitefish

**Per Serving:**

Calories: 256

Fat: 17.1 g

Protein: 23.5 g

Carbohydrate: 1.2 g

Calcium: 46 mg

Iron: 0.7 mg

Fiber: 0.1 g

Sodium: 686 mg

Cholesterol: 67 mg

*Whitefish, abundant in Canadian lakes, is marinated and then grilled for incredible flavor. If you don't have a fish basket, place fish between two well-greased wire cake racks and secure with thin wire.*

| | | |
|---|---|---|
| 1 | whole whitefish, cleaned (about 2 lb/1 kg) | 1 |
| 1 tsp | salt | 5 mL |
| 4 | slices lemon, halved | 4 |
| | Parsley sprigs | |

**Marinade:**

| | | |
|---|---|---|
| 1/4 cup | olive oil | 50 mL |
| 1/4 cup | lemon juice | 50 mL |
| 2 tbsp | Dijon mustard | 25 mL |
| 1 | clove garlic, minced | 1 |
| 4 tsp | chopped fresh oregano (or 2 tsp/ 10 mL dried) | 20 mL |
| Pinch | cayenne pepper | Pinch |

**Marinade:** In small bowl, whisk together olive oil, lemon juice, mustard, garlic, oregano and cayenne; set aside.

■ Rinse fish; pat dry inside and out with paper towels. Using scissors, remove all fins and trim tail. Remove head by slicing firmly through backbone.

■ Using sharp knife, cut diagonal scores about 4 inches (10 cm) long and 2 inches (5 cm) apart on each side of fish.

■ Sprinkle fish inside and out with salt. Stuff cavity with lemon slices and parsley sprigs. Loosely skewer base of fish closed.

■ Place fish in shallow porcelain or glass dish. Pour marinade over and turn fish to coat evenly. Cover and marinate for 30 minutes at room temperature or for up to 2 hours in refrigerator, turning occasionally.

■ Place fish in greased fish basket, reserving marinade. Place basket on greased grill 4 to 6 inches (10 to 15 cm) from medium-hot coals or on medium-high setting.

■ Cover with lid or tent with foil; grill fish for 10 minutes per inch (2.5 cm) of thickness or until flesh is opaque and flakes easily when tested with fork, basting occasionally with reserved marinade and turning fish over halfway through cooking time.

■ Carefully transfer fish to serving platter; remove skewers. Makes 4 servings.

**DELICIOUS FISH**

High in protein and low in fat, fish is one of the lightest main-dish meals you can serve — a serving of lean fish has about half the calories of an equal serving of most meats. Even salmon or trout, which contain some fat, have the polyunsaturated kind that may help in reducing the risk of heart disease.

Whether you serve it alone or add it to soups, stews, salads or sandwiches, fish is surprisingly versatile and easy to digest — one of the best reasons for serving it often.

*Grilled Whitefish*

# Grilled Shrimp

**Per Serving:**

Calories: 121

Fat: 4.7 g

Protein: 16.5 g

Carbohydrate: 3.4 g

Calcium: 60 mg

Iron: 1.4 mg

Fiber: 0.1 g

Sodium: 110 mg

Cholesterol: 94 mg

*For easy handling, thread shrimp on pairs of soaked wooden skewers, pushing skewers through ends of shrimp.*

| 1 lb | large shrimp | 500 g |
|------|-------------|-------|
| 2 tbsp | lime juice | 25 mL |
| 1/2 tsp | grated lime rind | 2 mL |
| 1 | clove garlic, minced | 1 |
| 1 tsp | minced gingerroot | 5 mL |
| 1 tbsp | sesame oil | 15 mL |
| 1 tbsp | vegetable oil | 15 mL |
| 1 tsp | coarsely cracked peppercorns | 5 mL |
| 2 tsp | liquid honey | 10 mL |

■ Using kitchen shears, cut each shrimp shell along back and devein, leaving shell and tail on shrimp. Rinse in cold water and pat dry.

■ In large bowl, combine lime juice and rind, garlic, ginger, sesame and vegetable oils, peppercorns and honey. Add shrimp, stirring to coat well. Cover and refrigerate for up to 30 minutes, turning shrimp occasionally.

■ Drain shrimp, reserving marinade. Thread onto greased metal or soaked wooden skewers, leaving a little space between each shrimp. Grill 4 inches (10 cm) from medium-hot coals or on medium-high setting or broil, brushing with reserved marinade, for 2 to 4 minutes per side or until pink and firm to the touch. Makes 4 servings.

*Grilled Shrimp*

## MENU SUGGESTION

TUNA FISHERMAN'S PIE
*This Page*

LIGHT COLESLAW
*Page 102*

FRESH PEARS

OATMEAL RAISIN COOKIES
*Page 126*

# Tuna Fisherman's Pie

**Per Serving:**

Calories: 309

Fat: 6.3 g

Protein: 28.7 g

Carbohydrate: 36.3 g

Calcium: 158 mg

Iron: 2.8 mg

Fiber: 6.5 g

Sodium: 925 mg

Cholesterol: 49 mg

*This satisfying meal-in-a-dish can be prepared ahead the same day and refrigerated; increase the cooking time by 10 to 15 minutes. And remember to use canned tuna packed in water — it's lower in fat.*

| | | |
|---|---|---|
| 1 tbsp | vegetable oil | 15 mL |
| 1/2 cup | chopped celery | 125 mL |
| 6 | green onions (white and pale green parts), sliced | 6 |
| 3 tbsp | all-purpose flour | 50 mL |
| 2 cups | vegetable or chicken stock | 500 mL |
| 1/4 tsp | cayenne pepper | 1 mL |
| | White pepper | |
| 1 cup | frozen peas | 250 mL |
| 1 | can (12 oz/341 mL) corn (undrained) | 1 |
| 1/4 cup | chopped fresh parsley | 50 mL |
| 2 | cans (each 7 oz/198 g) tuna, drained | 2 |
| 1 | egg white | 1 |
| 3 cups | mashed cooked potatoes | 750 mL |
| 1/2 cup | freshly grated Parmesan cheese | 50 mL |
| 1 tbsp | fine dry bread crumbs | 15 mL |

■ In nonstick saucepan, heat oil over medium heat; cook celery and onions, stirring, for 1 minute. Add 1 tbsp (15 mL) water and reduce heat to medium-low. Cover and cook for 4 minutes or until onions are tender-crisp.

■ Sprinkle with flour; cook, stirring, for 1 minute. Gradually blend in stock, cayenne pepper and 1/4 tsp (1 mL) white pepper; cook, stirring, over medium heat until thickened. Stir in peas, corn and parsley; remove from heat. Break tuna into chunks and add to vegetable mixture. Spoon into 10-cup or 9-inch (2.5 L) square baking dish.

■ In bowl, lightly beat egg white; gradually mix in potatoes until smooth. Stir in Parmesan cheese and pinch of white pepper. Spoon over tuna mixture and spread evenly; sprinkle with bread crumbs. Bake in 375°F (190°C) oven for 30 to 35 minutes or until golden brown and filling is bubbly. Makes 6 servings.

# Spinach-Pesto Fish Fillets

*This easy and versatile pesto is also delicious served over pasta.*

**Per Serving:**

Calories: 148

Fat: 7.6 g

Protein: 19 g

Carbohydrate: 1.6 g

Calcium: 64 mg

Iron: 1.2 mg

Fiber: 1.1 g

Sodium: 287 mg

Cholesterol: 58 mg

| | | |
|---|---|---|
| 1 cup | packed fresh spinach | 250 mL |
| 2 tbsp | toasted pine nuts or walnuts | 25 mL |
| 2 tbsp | freshly grated Parmesan cheese | 25 mL |
| 1 tbsp | olive oil | 15 mL |
| 1 | clove garlic, minced | 1 |
| 1/4 tsp | salt | 1 mL |
| | Pepper | |
| 1 lb | fish fillets (fresh or thawed) | 500 g |

■ In food processor or blender, combine spinach, pine nuts, cheese, olive oil, garlic, salt, and pepper to taste; process until well blended. Spread over fillets.

■ Starting at thin end, roll up fillets, jelly-roll style; secure with toothpicks. Arrange in single layer in greased shallow baking dish. Bake in 425°F (220°C) oven for about 10 minutes or until fish flakes easily when tested with fork. Remove toothpicks. Makes 4 servings.

## Cod Cakes

**Per Serving:**

Calories: 228

Fat: 2.9 g

Protein: 26.8 g

Carbohydrate: 23.6 g

Calcium: 152 mg

Iron: 1.4 mg

Fiber: 2 g

Sodium: 269 mg

Cholesterol: 61 mg

*Dijon mustard adds a lively nip to this low-fat entrée, which is good for those trying to cut down on salt as well.*

| | | |
|---|---|---|
| 3 | slices whole wheat bread | 3 |
| 1 tsp | margarine or butter | 5 mL |
| 1 lb | cod fillets (fresh or thawed) | 500 g |
| 1 cup | cubed cooked potato | 250 mL |
| 2 tbsp | minced onion | 25 mL |
| 1 tbsp | chopped fresh parsley | 15 mL |
| 1/2 tsp | Dijon mustard | 2 mL |
| Half | clove garlic | Half |
| 1/4 tsp | salt (optional) | 1 mL |
| 1/4 tsp | pepper | 1 mL |
| 1 | egg white | 1 |

**Sauce:**

| | | |
|---|---|---|
| 1 cup | low-fat yogurt | 250 mL |
| 1 tbsp | chopped fresh parsley | 15 mL |
| 1 tbsp | lemon juice | 15 mL |
| 2 tsp | grated lemon rind | 10 mL |

■ In food processor, process bread and margarine or butter until in crumbs; set aside. Cut fish into pieces.

■ In food processor and using on/off action, process cod, potato, onion, parsley, mustard, garlic, salt (if using) and pepper until coarsely chopped. Add egg white; process for 3 seconds or until mixed.

■ Using 1/4 cup (50 mL) mixture each, form into 12 patties; roll in crumbs. Bake on nonstick baking sheet in 400°F (200°C) oven for 12 to 15 minutes or until lightly browned.

**Sauce:** Combine yogurt, parsley, lemon juice and rind. Serve with cod cakes.

Makes 4 servings.

## Grilled Salmon Steaks

*To accompany this luscious salmon, parboil small red potatoes, then lightly brush potatoes and zucchini slices with oil and grill them until tender. Add steamed yellow and green beans and fresh cherry tomatoes to round out this delicious summer barbecue.*

| | | |
|---|---|---|
| 4 | salmon steaks, 1 inch (2.5 cm) thick (about 2 lb/1 kg total) | 4 |
| 1 tbsp | vegetable oil | 15 mL |
| | Yogurt Hollandaise (recipe follows) | |

**Per Serving (without hollandaise):**

Calories: 327

Fat: 15.5 g

Protein: 44.1 g

Carbohydrate: 0 g

Calcium: 207 mg

Iron: 2 mg

Fiber: 0 g

Sodium: 189 mg

Cholesterol: 77 mg

■ Brush salmon lightly with oil; grill on greased grill, 4 to 6 inches (10 to 15 cm) from medium-hot coals or at medium-high setting, turning once, for 10 minutes per inch (2.5 cm) of thickness or until fish flakes easily when tested with fork. Serve salmon with Yogurt Hollandaise. Makes 4 servings.

**Yogurt Hollandaise:**

| | | |
|---|---|---|
| 3/4 cup | low-fat yogurt | 175 mL |
| 2 | egg yolks | 2 |
| 1 tsp | cornstarch | 5 mL |
| 1 tsp | grainy mustard | 5 mL |
| 1 tsp | lemon juice | 5 mL |
| 1/4 tsp | salt | 1 mL |
| Pinch | each cayenne and white pepper | Pinch |
| 4 | green onions, chopped | 4 |

■ In top of double boiler, whisk together yogurt, egg yolks and cornstarch. Cook over simmering water, whisking constantly, for about 8 minutes or until thickened enough to coat spoon. Remove from heat; stir in mustard, lemon juice, salt, cayenne, white pepper and green onions. Set aside for up to 30 minutes. Makes 3/4 cup (175 mL) sauce.

*Per Tbsp (15 mL): 17 calories, 0.9 g fat, 1 g protein, 1.2 g carbohydrate, 27 mg calcium, 0.2 mg iron, 0.1 g fiber, 46 mg sodium, 28 mg cholesterol.*

*Grilled Salmon Steaks*

## Fish in a Packet

**Per Serving:**

Calories: 92

Fat: 0.9 g

Protein: 16.3 g

Carbohydrate: 4.3 g

Calcium: 22 mg

Iron: 0.7 mg

Fiber: 1.1 g

Sodium: 108 mg

Cholesterol: 54 mg

*Fish cooked in a packet requires no added fat and is sure to be moist. Serve with steamed zucchini and sliced tomatoes for a tasty low-calorie supper.*

| | | |
|---|---|---|
| 4 | **fish fillets (each about 4 oz/125 g)** | 4 |
| | **Salt and pepper** | |
| 1 tbsp | **orange juice** | 15 mL |
| 2 tsp | **prepared horseradish** | 10 mL |
| 1 | **large tomato, peeled, seeded and chopped** | 1 |
| 2 tbsp | **chopped onion** | 25 mL |
| 1/2 cup | **mixed sweet pepper strips** | 125 mL |
| 1 | **small carrot, julienned** | 1 |
| | **Minced fresh parsley** | |

■ Cut four 12-inch (30 cm) squares of foil; fold diagonally in half and open. Place each fillet on one half of foil. Season with salt and pepper to taste.

■ Mix orange juice with horseradish; spoon over fillets. Sprinkle evenly with tomato and onion. Surround each fillet with sweet pepper strips and carrots. Bring edges of foil together to form triangle and seal tightly. Bake on baking sheet in 450°F (230°C) oven for 10 to 15 minutes (depending on thickness of fillets) or until fish is opaque and flakes easily when tested with fork. Garnish with parsley. Makes 4 servings.

*Fish in a Packet*

## Grilled Teriyaki Fish Steaks with Yogurt-Caper Sauce

**Per Serving:**

Calories: 183

Fat: 5.9 g

Protein: 27.7 g

Carbohydrate: 2 g

Calcium: 53 mg

Iron: 1.4 mg

Fiber: 0 g

Sodium: 418 mg

Cholesterol: 77 mg

*Swordfish and salmon steaks are good choices for grilling because they hold their shape well, but any fresh fish steaks will do.*

| | | |
|---|---|---|
| 2 lb | fish steaks (about 3/4 inch/2 cm thick) | 1 kg |
| 3 tbsp | sherry | 50 mL |
| 2 tbsp | soy sauce | 25 mL |
| 2 tbsp | water | 25 mL |
| 1 tbsp | grated gingerroot | 15 mL |
| | Watercress sprigs | |

**Yogurt-Caper Sauce:**

| | | |
|---|---|---|
| 1/3 cup | low-fat yogurt | 75 mL |
| 1 tbsp | capers | 15 mL |
| 1 tbsp | chopped fresh parsley | 15 mL |
| 1 tsp | minced sweet pickle | 5 mL |
| | Salt and pepper | |

■ Place fish steaks in single layer in 13- x 9-inch (3.5 L) baking dish. Combine sherry, soy sauce, water and gingerroot; pour over fish. Cover and refrigerate for 2 hours or up to 1 day, turning once or twice.

■ Grill fish on greased grill over medium-hot coals or on medium setting for 3 to 4 minutes on each side or until fish is opaque and flakes easily when tested with fork.

**Yogurt-Caper Sauce:** In bowl, combine yogurt, capers, parsley, pickle, and salt and pepper to taste.

■ Top each serving of fish with dollop of sauce. Garnish with watercress. Makes 6 servings.

**MENU SUGGESTION**

FISH FILLETS CASINO
*This Page*

FETTUCINE NOODLES

TROPICAL FRUIT SALAD
*Page 120*

## Fish Fillets Casino

*Any firm-flesh white fish (sole, haddock or cod) is great in this recipe.*

**Per Serving:**

Calories: 116

Fat: 2.8 g

Protein: 18 g

Carbohydrate: 3.8 g

Calcium: 23 mg

Iron: 0.7 mg

Fiber: 0.7 g

Sodium: 176 mg

Cholesterol: 60 mg

| | | |
|---|---|---|
| 1 lb | fish fillets (fresh or thawed) | 500 g |
| 2 | slices bacon, diced | 2 |
| 1 | onion, minced | 1 |
| 1/2 cup | each chopped sweet green and red pepper | 125 mL |
| 1 tsp | lemon juice | 5 mL |
| 1 tsp | sherry (optional) | 5 mL |
| 1/2 tsp | Worcestershire sauce | 2 mL |
| Dash | hot pepper sauce | Dash |
| | Salt and pepper | |
| 1 tbsp | dry bread crumbs | 15 mL |

■ Arrange fish fillets in single layer in greased baking dish.

■ In small saucepan, cook bacon over medium heat, stirring occasionally, for about 3 minutes or until golden. Add onion and cook, stirring often, for about 2 minutes or until softened. Add green and red peppers; cook, stirring, for 1 minute. Remove from heat.

■ Add lemon juice, sherry (if using), Worcestershire, hot pepper sauce, and salt and pepper to taste; spoon over fillets. Sprinkle with bread crumbs. Bake in 425°F (220°C) oven for about 10 minutes or until fish flakes easily when tested with fork. Makes 4 servings.

## Seafood Pasta

**Per Serving:**

Calories: 476

Fat: 6.2 g

Protein: 31 g

Carbohydrate: 71 g

Calcium: 120 mg

Iron: 3.4 mg

Fiber: 3.1 g

Sodium: 230 mg

Cholesterol: 73 mg

*Choose a long, narrow pasta like spaghetti, linguine or fettucine for this recipe. Saffron adds a subtle flavor but can be omitted, if desired.*

| | | |
|---|---|---|
| 1/2 cup | dry white wine | 125 mL |
| 1/2 cup | chicken stock | 125 mL |
| 2 | shallots, minced | 2 |
| 1 | clove garlic, minced | 1 |
| 1 | tomato, peeled, seeded and diced | 1 |
| 2 tsp | tomato paste | 10 mL |
| Pinch | powdered saffron | Pinch |
| 1/3 lb | halibut, monkfish or turbot, cut in 1-inch (2.5 cm) pieces | 170 g |
| 1/3 lb | shrimp, peeled and deveined | 170 g |
| 1/3 lb | scallops | 170 g |
| 1 tbsp | cornstarch | 15 mL |
| 1/2 cup | light cream | 125 mL |
| | Salt and pepper | |
| 3/4 lb | pasta, cooked | 375 g |
| 1/4 cup | chopped fresh parsley | 50 mL |

■ In skillet, combine wine, chicken stock, shallots, garlic, tomato, tomato paste and saffron; bring to simmer over medium heat and cook for 2 minutes. Add fish, shrimp and scallops; cover and simmer for 3 minutes or until shrimp are pink and fish and scallops are opaque. With slotted spoon, remove fish and seafood to bowl; set aside and keep warm.

■ Dissolve cornstarch in 1 tbsp (15 mL) of the cream and add to skillet along with remaining cream; cook, stirring, until boiling and thickened. Return fish and seafood to skillet and stir to coat; season with salt and pepper to taste. Spoon over pasta and sprinkle with parsley. Makes 4 servings.

## Pasta with Tomatoes, Black Olives and Two Cheeses

*For the very best flavor, use Balsamic vinegar and calamata olives. Choose pastas such as penne, rigatoni, fusilli or medium shells.*

**Per Serving:**

Calories: 518

Fat: 16.7 g

Protein: 17.5 g

Carbohydrate: 76 g

Calcium: 202 mg

Iron: 2.9 mg

Fiber: 5.5 g

Sodium: 562 mg

Cholesterol: 12 mg

| | | |
|---|---|---|
| 12 oz | penne | 375 g |
| 2 tbsp | olive oil | 25 mL |
| 1 | small leek (white and pale green part), thinly sliced | 1 |
| 2 | cloves garlic, minced | 2 |
| 1/4 cup | torn fresh basil | 50 mL |
| 2 tbsp | freshly grated Parmesan cheese | 25 mL |
| 2 tsp | Balsamic or red wine vinegar | 10 mL |
| | Pepper | |
| 4 | tomatoes, cut in wedges | 4 |
| 1/3 cup | halved black olives | 75 mL |
| 1/2 cup | crumbled Asiago cheese | 125 mL |

■ In large pot of boiling water, cook pasta until tender but firm; drain, then return to pot to keep warm.

■ Meanwhile, in a small nonstick skillet, heat oil over medium-low heat; cook leek and garlic, covered and stirring occasionally, for 5 to 7 minutes or until leek is softened and almost transparent. Add to pasta along with basil, Parmesan cheese, vinegar, and pepper to taste; toss gently to mix.

■ Add tomatoes and olives; toss gently. Sprinkle with Asiago cheese. Makes 4 servings.

*Seafood Pasta*

**MENU SUGGESTION**

PENNE WITH RED PEPPER SAUCE
*This Page*

CELERY HEARTS AND BLACK OLIVES

SESAME BREAD STICKS

BLUEBERRY CUSTARD PARFAITS
*Page 124*

# Spinach Fettuccine with Cauliflower and Anchovy Sauce

*The rich flavors of olive oil, garlic and anchovies blend subtly with cauliflower and Parmesan cheese to make a delightful sauce.*

| | | |
|---|---|---|
| 4 cups | cauliflower florets (about half a head) | 1 L |
| 3 tbsp | olive oil | 50 mL |
| 1 | clove garlic, minced | 1 |
| 4 | anchovy fillets, minced (or 2 tsp/10 mL anchovy paste) | 4 |
| 3/4 lb | spinach fettuccine | 375 g |
| 2 tbsp | margarine or butter | 25 mL |
| 1/3 cup | freshly grated Parmesan cheese | 75 mL |
| | Pepper | |

**Per Serving:**

Calories: 516

Fat: 19.5 g

Protein: 16.1 g

Carbohydrate: 68.8 g

Calcium: 152 mg

Iron: 1.9 mg

Fiber: 4 g

Sodium: 232 mg

Cholesterol: 7 mg

■ Steam cauliflower for about 3 minutes or until tender-crisp.

■ In large skillet, heat oil over medium heat; cook garlic for 1 minute. Add anchovies and cook, stirring, for 2 minutes. Remove from heat.

■ In large pot of boiling salted water, cook spinach fettuccine until tender but firm. Drain and transfer to skillet along with cooked cauliflower florets and margarine or butter; toss well. Add Parmesan and season with pepper to taste; toss thoroughly. Transfer to warmed serving bowl. Makes 4 servings.

# Penne with Red Pepper Sauce

**Per Serving:**

Calories: 417

Fat: 12.3 g

Protein: 16.2 g

Carbohydrate: 59.6 g

Calcium: 216 mg

Iron: 1.5 mg

Fiber: 3.6 g

Sodium: 272 mg

Cholesterol: 14 mg

*Toss sweet red pepper sauce with hot pasta or serve over broiled fish. To use as a dip for vegetables, blend equal amounts of sauce and light mayonnaise.*

| | | |
|---|---|---|
| 1 | sweet red pepper | 1 |
| 1 | clove garlic, chopped | 1 |
| 1/2 cup | freshly grated Parmesan cheese | 125 mL |
| 1 tbsp | ground almonds | 15 mL |
| 1 tbsp | olive oil | 15 mL |
| 1 tbsp | light cream cheese | 15 mL |
| Dash | hot pepper sauce | Dash |
| | Salt and pepper | |
| 1/2 lb | penne, cooked | 250 g |
| | Fresh basil leaves | |

■ On baking sheet, roast red pepper in 375°F (190°C) oven for about 30 minutes or until puffed and lightly browned. Let cool; peel and seed.

■ In food processor or blender, purée garlic. With motor running, blend in red pepper, half of the Parmesan cheese, the almonds, oil, cream cheese and hot pepper sauce. Season with salt and pepper to taste.

■ Toss sauce with penne. Sprinkle with remaining Parmesan; garnish with basil. Makes 3 servings.

# Light Spaghetti Sauce

**Per Serving**
**(with pasta):**

Calories: 502

Fat: 4.9 g

Protein: 21 g

Carbohydrate: 92.4 g

Calcium: 76 mg

Iron: 3.3 mg

Fiber: 6.3 g

Sodium: 186 mg

Cholesterol: 14 mg

*Allow 4 oz (125 g) of pasta per serving; freeze any extra sauce.*

| | | |
|---|---|---|
| 1/2 lb | lean ground beef | 250 g |
| 2 cups | finely chopped mushrooms | 500 mL |
| 1 | onion, finely chopped | 1 |
| 1 | clove garlic, minced | 1 |
| 1 | can (28 oz/796 mL) tomatoes | 1 |
| 2 tbsp | tomato paste | 25 mL |
| 1 tsp | packed brown sugar | 5 mL |
| 1 tsp | dried oregano | 5 mL |
| 1 tsp | dried basil | 5 mL |
| 1/2 tsp | dried thyme | 2 mL |
| 1 | bay leaf | 1 |
| 1/4 cup | chopped fresh parsley | 50 mL |
| | Salt and pepper | |

■ Over medium-high heat, cook beef, mushrooms, onion and garlic, stirring often, for 8 to 10 minutes or until liquid has almost evaporated.

■ Stir in tomatoes (breaking up with back of spoon), tomato paste, sugar, oregano, basil, thyme and bay leaf; bring to boil. Reduce heat and simmer for 15 to 20 minutes or until thickened. Remove bay leaf. Stir in parsley, and salt and pepper to taste. Makes 8 servings.

**Here's a handy guide to the different uses and shapes of pasta.**
**With sauces, meat, fish, vegetables and cheese dishes: use noodles, spaghetti and linguine.**
**In casseroles: use lasagna, rigatoni and gnocchi.**
**With delicate sauces and in salads: use spaghettini, conchiglie (medium-sized shells) and penne (hollow spears).**
**For stuffing with meat or cheese mixtures: use manicotti, cannelloni and jumbo shells.**
**For soups: use tiny pasta bow ties, stars, letters of the alphabet and shells.**

# Rotini with Spicy Tomato Clam Sauce

*With lots of flavor and a pleasant spiciness, this quick skillet dish will soon become a sophisticated favorite. Serve it with a vinaigrette-dressed salad of leafy greens.*

**Per Serving:**

Calories: 470

Fat: 12 g

Protein: 15.9 g

Carbohydrate: 75.1 g

Calcium: 126 mg

Iron: 4.5 mg

Fiber: 6.5 g

Sodium: 670 mg

Cholesterol: 12 mg

| | | |
|---|---|---|
| 2 tbsp | olive oil | 25 mL |
| 3 | cloves garlic, minced | 3 |
| 1 tsp | anchovy paste | 5 mL |
| 1/4 tsp | hot pepper flakes | 1 mL |
| 1 | can (28 oz/796 mL) tomatoes (undrained) | 1 |
| 1 | can (5 oz/142 g) baby clams | 1 |
| 1/4 tsp | pepper | 1 mL |
| 1/3 cup | chopped fresh parsley | 75 mL |
| 1/2 cup | black olives, pitted and coarsely chopped | 125 mL |
| 5 cups | rotini (3/4 lb/375 g) | 1.25 L |

■ In large skillet, heat oil over medium-low heat; cook garlic for about 4 minutes or until softened but not browned. Remove from heat.

■ Stir in anchovy paste and hot pepper flakes. Add tomatoes, juice from clams and pepper; return to medium heat and bring to simmer, breaking up tomatoes with wooden spoon. Simmer, uncovered and stirring often, for about 20 minutes or until thickened.

■ Add clams and half of the parsley; simmer for 2 minutes. Stir in olives; simmer for 2 minutes.

■ Meanwhile, in large pot of boiling salted water, cook pasta until tender but firm. Drain well and toss with sauce. Sprinkle each serving with remaining parsley. Makes 4 servings.

**MENU SUGGESTION**

POLENTA PIZZA CASSEROLE
*This Page*

ROMAINE with
CREAMY BUTTERMILK DRESSING
*Page 98*

BERRIES with
ORANGE CREAM TOPPING
*Page 122*

# Polenta Pizza Casserole

**Per Serving:**

Calories: 241

Fat: 9.4 g

Protein: 18.8 g

Carbohydrate: 20.4 g

Calcium: 306 mg

Iron: 1.4 mg

Fiber: 1.3 g

Sodium: 1378 mg

Cholesterol: 39 mg

*Be sure to let this colorful meal in one dish stand for 5 minutes for easy slicing. If you want to cut down on the sodium in this recipe, omit the salt and use homemade tomato sauce instead of canned.*

| | | |
|---|---|---|
| 1-3/4 cups | water | 425 mL |
| 1/2 cup | cornmeal | 125 mL |
| 1/2 tsp | salt | 2 mL |
| 1 cup | tomato sauce | 250 mL |
| 1/2 tsp | dried basil | 2 mL |
| 4 | slices lean back bacon | 4 |
| Half | sweet green pepper, diced | Half |
| 1 cup | sliced mushrooms | 250 mL |
| | Pepper | |
| 1-1/2 cups | shredded part-skim-milk mozzarella cheese | 375 mL |

■ In saucepan, combine water, cornmeal and salt; bring to boil, stirring. Cover and reduce heat to medium; cook for 5 to 8 minutes or until thickened and smooth, stirring occasionally.

■ Transfer to lightly greased deep 9-inch (23 cm) glass pie plate; smooth top. Combine tomato sauce and basil; spread on top. Set aside.

■ Coarsely chop bacon. In nonstick skillet, cook bacon over medium heat for 1 minute. Add green pepper and mushrooms; cook, stirring, for 2 to 3 minutes or just until mushrooms are tender. Season with pepper to taste.

*Polenta Pizza Casserole*

■ Spoon vegetable mixture evenly over tomato sauce; sprinkle with cheese. Bake in 350°F (180°C) oven for 20 minutes or until cheese is melted and bubbly. Let stand for 5 minutes. Makes 4 servings.

**Microwave method:**

■ In 8-cup (2 L) microwaveable casserole, combine water, cornmeal and salt; cover and microwave at High for 5 to 7 minutes or until thickened and bubbly, stirring twice. Smooth top and set aside.

■ On rack or paper-towel-lined plate, arrange bacon in single layer; cover with paper towel and microwave at High for 4 minutes or until crisp. Crumble bacon and set aside.

■ Stir together tomato sauce and basil; spread evenly over cornmeal mixture. Scatter bacon, green pepper and mushrooms evenly over top; season with pepper to taste.

■ Cover with waxed paper and microwave at High for 5 minutes or until vegetables are tender-crisp, rotating once. Sprinkle with cheese; cover with foil and let stand for 5 minutes or until cheese melts. Makes 4 servings.

**WHO SAYS PASTA IS FATTENING?**

If you've always thought that pasta and other carbohydrate foods like breads and grains are fattening — think again!

Carbohydrates function as the primary energy source for the human body. There are two kinds of carbohydrates. The simple ones like sugar and honey are sweet — they provide instant energy. The complex ones are the starches found in pasta and other foods like breads, cereals, grains, fruits and vegetables. Since they take longer to digest, complex carbohydrates give us a longer-lasting source of energy.

But a word of warning: what you serve *on* or *with* the pasta is important. Don't add a lot of fat (rich creams, butters, cheeses) and make a healthy food less healthy.

# Make It Meatless

**Y**ou'll never miss the meat when you serve these flavorful meatless dishes. Whether it's Lean and Fast Vegetable Lasagna or Bulgur-Stuffed Cabbage Rolls with Tomato Coulis, each of these appetizing recipes is a satisfying, low-fat alternative to meat — and each provides essential vitamins, minerals, fiber and protein for a healthy diet. What's more, these meatless dishes are an easy, delicious way to add more garden-fresh vegetables, fiber-rich legumes, and protein-rich eggs and cheese to your diet.

## Bulgur-Stuffed Cabbage Rolls

**Per Serving:**

Calories: 207

Fat: 4.6 g

Protein: 8.4 g

Carbohydrate: 37.5 g

Calcium: 123 mg

Iron: 3.3 mg

Fiber: 8 g

Sodium: 99 mg

Cholesterol: 57 mg

*If desired, omit the tomato coulis and simmer these light yet satisfying cabbage rolls in tomato sauce.*

| | | |
|---|---|---|
| 1 | head cabbage | 1 |
| Half | Bulgur Pilaf recipe (recipe, p.84) | Half |
| 1 | egg, slightly beaten | 1 |
| 1/4 cup | vegetable stock | 50 mL |
| **Tomato Coulis:** | | |
| 5 cups | chopped seeded peeled tomatoes | 1.25 L |
| 2 tbsp | chopped fresh dill | 25 mL |
| | Salt and pepper | |
| **Garnish:** | | |
| | Light sour cream | |
| | Dill sprigs | |

■ Trim and core cabbage. In large deep saucepan, cover cabbage with boiling water; let stand for 10 minutes or until outer leaves are easy to remove. Remove 8 leaves, dipping cabbage in boiling water if necessary to soften leaves; set leaves aside.

■ Finely chop enough of the remaining cabbage to make 2 cups (500 mL); return to saucepan and cook in lightly salted boiling water just until tender. Drain and stir into Bulgur Pilaf along with egg.

■ Spoon bulgur mixture evenly onto each cabbage leaf; roll up, folding in sides, to make neat package. Place seam side down in Dutch oven or deep skillet; pour in vegetable stock. Bring to simmer; cover and cook over medium-low heat for 30 to 35 minutes or until cabbage rolls are tender throughout.

**Tomato Coulis:** Meanwhile, in food processor or blender, purée tomatoes; transfer to small saucepan and gently heat through. Stir in dill; season with salt and pepper to taste.

**Garnish:** Spoon tomato coulis onto 4 plates; top each with 2 cabbage rolls. Garnish rolls with dollop of sour cream and sprig of dill. Makes 4 servings.

*Bulgur-Stuffed Cabbage Rolls*

## Bulgur Pilaf

**Per Serving:**

Calories: 199

Fat: 3.6 g

Protein: 5.4 g

Carbohydrate: 37.9 g

Calcium: 39 mg

Iron: 2.3 mg

Fiber: 4.9 g

Sodium: 51 mg

Cholesterol: 0 mg

*This versatile pilaf makes an appetizing side dish or use it to stuff lightly blanched cabbage or grape leaves (see recipe for Bulgur-Stuffed Cabbage Rolls, p.82).*

| | | |
|---|---|---|
| 1 tbsp | margarine or butter | 15 mL |
| 1 | onion, chopped | 1 |
| 1 | clove garlic, minced | 1 |
| 1 | stalk celery, chopped | 1 |
| 2 cups | vegetable stock | 500 mL |
| 1/2 tsp | dried thyme | 2 mL |
| 1 cup | bulgur | 250 mL |
| 2 tbsp | currants | 25 mL |
| 1/4 cup | chopped fresh parsley | 50 mL |
| | Salt and pepper | |

■ In saucepan, melt margarine or butter over medium-low heat; stir in onion, garlic and celery to coat. Add 1 tbsp (15 mL) of the stock; cover and cook, stirring occasionally, over medium-low heat for 5 minutes or until onion is softened. Add remaining stock and thyme; bring to simmer. Add bulgur and cook, covered, for 15 to 20 minutes or until bulgur is tender and most of the stock is absorbed.

■ Stir in currants; let stand, covered, for 5 minutes. Stir in parsley, and salt and pepper to taste. Makes 4 servings.

### Microwave method:

■ In 4-cup (1 L) measure, combine vegetable stock and thyme; microwave at High for 3 to 4 minutes or until simmering. Set aside.

■ In 12-cup (3 L) casserole, combine margarine or butter, onion, garlic and celery; cover and microwave at High for 2 minutes.

■ Add hot stock, bulgur and currants; cover and microwave at High for 4 to 5 minutes or until boiling. Microwave at Medium (50%) for 7 to 9 minutes or until bulgur is almost tender and most of the liquid is absorbed, rotating dish once.

■ Let pilaf stand, covered, for 10 minutes. Stir in parsley; season with salt and pepper to taste. Makes 4 servings.

## Easy Tomato Sauce

*Cook 3/4 lb (375 g) penne or spaghetti to serve with this sauce and pass 1/2 cup (125 mL) freshly grated Parmesan cheese separately.*

| | | |
|---|---|---|
| 2 tbsp | vegetable oil | 25 mL |
| 1 | large onion, chopped | 1 |
| 2 | cloves garlic, minced | 2 |
| 1/4 cup | finely chopped carrot | 50 mL |
| 1 | can (28 oz/796 mL) tomatoes (undrained) | 1 |
| 1 | bay leaf | 1 |
| 1/2 tsp | each dried basil and oregano | 2 mL |
| 1/4 tsp | granulated sugar | 1 mL |
| | Salt and pepper | |
| 1/4 cup | minced fresh parsley | 50 mL |

■ In large skillet, heat oil over medium heat; cook onion, garlic and carrot until softened, about 5 minutes.

■ Add tomatoes, mashing with fork into small chunks. Stir in bay leaf, basil, oregano and sugar; bring to boil. Reduce heat and simmer, uncovered, for 20 to 30 minutes or until thickened. Season with salt and pepper to taste. Stir in parsley. Remove bay leaf. Makes enough for 4 servings.

**Per Serving:**

Calories: 122

Fat: 7.4 g

Protein: 2.6 g

Carbohydrate: 13.5 g

Calcium: 79 mg

Iron: 1.8 mg

Fiber: 3.4 g

Sodium: 343 mg

Cholesterol: 0 mg

### QUINOA — THE SUPER GRAIN OF THE FUTURE

Satisfying but light — not sticky or heavy — easy to digest and quick cooking, quinoa (pronounced keen-wa) offers more protein than any other grain. It's a good source of fiber and has only 107 calories per 1/2 to 3/4 cup (125 to 175 mL) cooked. You can substitute quinoa for any grain in any recipe or use it on its own as you would rice. Look for it in your favorite health food store.

# Tex-Mex Frittata

**Per Serving:**

Calories: 236

Fat: 10.3 g

Protein: 15.8 g

Carbohydrate: 20.6 g

Calcium: 194 mg

Iron: 1.2 mg

Fiber: 2 g

Sodium: 564 mg

Cholesterol: 162 mg

*Browned potatoes and onions form a "crust" for the eggs and tomatoes. You can use any fresh hot pepper or pickled or canned jalapeño. If using fresh peppers, wear rubber gloves to seed and chop them.*

| 2 | potatoes, peeled | 2 |
|---|---|---|
| 4 tsp | vegetable oil | 20 mL |
| 1/2 cup | chopped onions | 125 mL |
| | Salt and pepper | |
| 3 | eggs | 3 |
| 3 | egg whites | 3 |
| 2 | tomatoes, seeded and chopped | 2 |
| 1 tbsp | chopped jalapeño pepper | 15 mL |
| 1 cup | shredded low-fat Cheddar or Monterey Jack cheese | 250 mL |

■ In saucepan of boiling salted water, cook potatoes for 8 to 10 minutes or until tender. Drain and refresh under cold running water; drain and dice.

■ In ovenproof skillet, heat oil over medium heat; cook potatoes and onions, stirring occasionally, for 6 to 8 minutes or until browned. Season with salt and pepper to taste. Lightly pat down potato mixture to level.

■ Beat together eggs and egg whites; pour over potato mixture. Season with pepper to taste. Cover and cook over medium-low heat for 6 to 8 minutes or until eggs are set. Sprinkle with tomatoes and jalapeño pepper; top with cheese and broil for 2 minutes or until cheese is melted and lightly browned. Cut into wedges to serve. Makes 4 servings.

*Tex-Mex Frittata*

(left) Tabouli

# Tabouli (Parsley and Bulgur Salad)

| 1/2 tsp | pepper | 2 mL |
|---------|--------|------|
| | Romaine lettuce | |

**Per Serving:**

Calories: 134

Fat: 7.3 g

Protein: 3.5 g

Carbohydrate: 16.1 g

Calcium: 89 mg

Iron: 3.9 mg

Fiber: 4.1 g

Sodium: 478 mg

Cholesterol: 0 mg

*Parsley is the vital ingredient in this refreshing, light salad. Be sure to chop it by hand instead of in a machine; otherwise, it will release too much moisture and make the tabouli watery.*

| 1/2 cup | bulgur | 125 mL |
|---------|--------|--------|
| 6 | sprigs fresh mint | 6 |
| 1 | bunch green onions | 1 |
| 3 | bunches parsley | 3 |
| 5 | tomatoes, chopped | 5 |
| 1/4 cup | olive oil | 50 mL |
| 1/4 cup | lemon juice | 50 mL |
| 1 tsp | salt | 5 mL |

■ Rinse bulgur; soak in cold water for about 1 hour or until softened and expanded. Drain well.

■ Meanwhile, chop mint and green onions finely; place in large bowl. Chop parsley to make 5 cups (1.25 L); add to bowl along with bulgur and 4 of the tomatoes.

■ Stir together oil, lemon juice, salt and pepper; drizzle over parsley mixture and toss. Taste and adjust seasoning if necessary. Garnish with remaining tomato. Surround with lettuce leaves to scoop up tabouli. Makes 8 servings.

**MENU SUGGESTION**

STIR-FRIED TOFU AND
VEGETABLES WITH OYSTER SAUCE
*This Page*

HOT FLUFFY RICE

LETTUCE WEDGES with
ORIENTAL VINAIGRETTE
*Page 98*

JAPANESE PEARS

# Stir-Fried Tofu and Vegetables with Oyster Sauce

**Per Serving:**

Calories: 190

Fat: 12.2 g

Protein: 10.5 g

Carbohydrate: 12.2 g

Calcium: 420 mg

Iron: 7.4 mg

Fiber: 1.9 g

Sodium: 264 mg

Cholesterol: 0 mg

*Serve this colorful stir-fry on hot rice for a quick and low-cal meatless main dish. If you use a nonstick skillet, you need only 1 tbsp (15 mL) vegetable oil.*

| | | |
|---|---|---|
| 1/2 lb | tofu | 250 g |
| 6 | green onions | 6 |
| 4 | stalks celery | 4 |
| 1 | sweet red pepper | 1 |
| 1/4 cup | water | 50 mL |
| 2 tbsp | oyster sauce | 25 mL |
| 1 tbsp | cornstarch | 15 mL |
| 1 tbsp | dry sherry or mirin (rice wine for cooking) | 15 mL |
| 1 tbsp | soy sauce | 15 mL |
| 2 tbsp | vegetable oil | 25 mL |
| 1 tbsp | minced gingerroot | 15 mL |
| 2 cups | sliced mushrooms (about 1/4 lb/125 g) | 500 mL |

■ Drain tofu and weigh down to press for 30 minutes. Cut into 1/2-inch (1 cm) cubes; set aside.

■ Cut onions and celery into 1/2-inch (1 cm) diagonal pieces. Cut red pepper into 1/2-inch (1 cm) chunks. Set vegetables aside.

■ Stir together water, oyster sauce, cornstarch, sherry and soy sauce; set aside.

■ In wok or large heavy skillet, heat 1 tbsp (15 mL) of the oil over high heat; stir-fry gingerroot for 30 seconds. Add tofu and cook, stirring gently, for about 3 minutes or until light brown. With slotted spoon, transfer to heated platter.

■ Add remaining oil to wok and heat; stir-fry mushrooms, onions, celery and red pepper for 1 minute. Return tofu to wok; stir to mix well. Stir oyster sauce mixture; pour into wok and cook, stirring, until liquid comes to boil and boils for 1 minute. Serve immediately. Makes 4 servings.

**TOFU TIPS**

■ Tofu is cholesterol-free, high in calcium and protein and low in calories and saturated fats.

■ Tofu is sold in 1-lb (500 g) water-packed cakes in sealed plastic cartons. It can be found in the produce section of most supermarkets or in health food stores. Remember to check the ''best before'' date on the carton.

■ Tofu must always be covered with fresh water to prevent a thick skin from forming. Remember to change the water daily and store the tofu in the refrigerator.

■ Tofu comes in two forms: soft and firm. Use soft tofu for blending into sauces, salad dressings, cream soups and dessert toppings. Firm tofu holds its shape better and is best for stir-fries.

■ Drain tofu in a sieve before using. For firmer tofu, drain in a colander, covered and set over a bowl, in the refrigerator for up to 12 hours.

**MENU SUGGESTION**

LENTIL SHEPHERD'S PIE
*This Page*

SPINACH SALAD with
CREAMY BUTTERMILK DRESSING
*Page 98*

# Lentil Shepherd's Pie

**Per Serving:**

Calories: 231

Fat: 3.3 g

Protein: 13.4 g

Carbohydrate: 40.5 g

Calcium: 113 mg

Iron: 3.1 mg

Fiber: 6.2 g

Sodium: 854 mg

Cholesterol: 5 mg

*If desired, use dried green lentils instead of canned by simmering 1 cup (250 mL) rinsed lentils with about 5 cups (1.25 L) water for 25 minutes or until tender, then draining well.*

| | | |
|---|---|---|
| 2 tsp | vegetable oil | 10 mL |
| 1 | onion, chopped | 1 |
| 2 | carrots, chopped | 2 |
| 2 | cloves garlic, minced | 2 |
| 1 | can (19 oz/540 mL) stewed tomatoes | 1 |
| 1 | can (19 oz/540 mL) green lentils, drained and rinsed | 1 |
| | Pepper | |
| 3 cups | mashed potatoes (about 3 large) | 750 mL |
| 1 cup | low-fat cottage cheese | 250 mL |
| 4 | green onions, chopped | 4 |
| | Salt | |

■ In large skillet, heat oil over medium heat; cook onion, carrots and garlic, stirring occasionally, for 3 to 5 minutes or until softened.

■ Add tomatoes and mash with potato masher; bring to boil. Reduce heat to medium and cook, uncovered, for 15 to 20 minutes or until thickened. Stir in lentils; season with pepper to taste. Transfer to deep 8-cup (2 L) baking dish.

■ Combine potatoes, cottage cheese and green onions; season with salt and pepper to taste. Spoon over lentil mixture, covering completely; bake, uncovered, in 400°F (200°C) oven for 35 minutes or until heated through. Makes 6 servings.

# Spaghetti with Eggplant and Tomatoes

*Leave the peel on the eggplant to increase the fiber in this hearty sauce.*

| | | |
|---|---|---|
| 1 | eggplant (about 1 lb/500 g) | 1 |
| 1 tsp | salt | 5 mL |
| 2 tbsp | olive oil | 25 mL |
| 1 | large onion, chopped | 1 |
| 2 | cloves garlic, minced | 2 |
| 5 | tomatoes, peeled, seeded and chopped (2-1/2 cups/625 mL) | 5 |
| 1 tsp | dried basil | 5 mL |
| 1/4 tsp | crushed fennel seeds (optional) | 1 mL |
| | Pepper | |
| 3/4 lb | spaghetti or linguine | 375 g |
| 2 tbsp | freshly grated Parmesan cheese | 25 mL |
| 1/4 cup | chopped fresh parsley | 50 mL |

**Per Serving:**

Calories: 443

Fat: 9 g

Protein: 13.9 g

Carbohydrate: 77.5 g

Calcium: 95 mg

Iron: 2.7 mg

Fiber: 6.7 g

Sodium: 65 mg

Cholesterol: 2 mg

■ Peel eggplant and cut into 1-inch (2.5 cm) cubes. Place in single layer in colander and sprinkle with salt. Let stand for 30 minutes; rinse and drain well. Pat dry.

■ In large heavy saucepan or deep nonstick skillet, heat oil over medium-high heat; sauté eggplant, stirring, until golden and partly softened, about 5 minutes. With slotted spoon, remove eggplant to bowl and set aside.

■ Reduce heat to medium; add onion and garlic and cook, stirring, for 1 minute. Return eggplant to pan along with tomatoes, basil and fennel seeds (if using); reduce heat and simmer, covered, for 15 minutes or until eggplant is tender. Season with pepper to taste.

■ Meanwhile, in large pot of boiling water, cook spaghetti until tender but firm. Drain well and toss with tomato sauce. Transfer to warmed serving bowl; sprinkle with Parmesan, then parsley. Makes 4 servings.

# Vegetable Curry

**Per Serving**
(without
couscous):

Calories: 161

Fat: 3.5 g

Protein: 4.9 g

Carbohydrate: 29.3 g

Calcium: 59 mg

Iron: 2.1 mg

Fiber: 5.3 g

Sodium: 208 mg

Cholesterol: 0 mg

*You'll never miss the meat when you serve this colorful curry dish. Spooned over fluffy heaps of couscous and served with chick-peas, it provides a complete protein. Offer chopped fresh mango, a cucumber and yogurt salad and chutney as a flavorful accompaniment.*

| | | |
|---|---|---|
| 1 tbsp | vegetable oil | 15 mL |
| 1 | onion, coarsely chopped | 1 |
| 4 | cloves garlic, minced | 4 |
| 1 | large sweet potato, peeled and cubed | 1 |
| 2 | carrots, sliced | 2 |
| 1 | hot banana pepper, seeded and finely chopped | 1 |
| 4 tsp | curry powder | 20 mL |
| 1 cup | vegetable stock | 250 mL |
| 1 | yellow zucchini | 1 |
| 1 | sweet red pepper | 1 |
| 1 cup | cut green beans | 250 mL |
| 1 cup | drained canned chick-peas | 250 mL |
| 2 tsp | lime juice | 10 mL |
| | Salt and pepper | |
| | Couscous (sidebar, this page) | |

■ In nonstick Dutch oven or large saucepan, heat oil over medium heat; cook onion and garlic, covered, for 3 to 5 minutes or until softened.

■ Add sweet potato, carrots, hot banana pepper and curry powder; cook, stirring, for 2 minutes or until fragrant. Stir in stock; cover and simmer, stirring occasionally, for 8 minutes or until vegetables are tender-crisp.

■ Meanwhile, cut zucchini into thick finger-length strips. Seed red pepper and cut into 1/2-inch (1 cm) wide strips. Add zucchini, red pepper and green beans to pan and return to simmer; cover and cook for 5 minutes or until tender-crisp. Stir in chick-peas and lime juice and heat through. Season with salt and pepper to taste. Serve over couscous. Makes 6 servings.

# Lentil and Wild Rice Pilaf

*In this pilaf recipe, use brown rice if wild rice is unavailable. If you can't find the rice-shaped pasta called orzo, just omit it or use another small pasta shape.*

| | | |
|---|---|---|
| 2 tbsp | margarine or butter | 25 mL |
| 1 | onion, diced | 1 |
| 1 | clove garlic, minced | 1 |
| 1 tsp | curry powder | 5 mL |
| 1 cup | green lentils, rinsed | 250 mL |
| 1/2 cup | wild rice, rinsed | 125 mL |
| 1/2 cup | orzo | 125 mL |
| 3 cups | chicken or vegetable stock | 750 mL |
| | Salt and pepper | |

**Per Serving:**

Calories: 273

Fat: 5.2 g

Protein: 15 g

Carbohydrate: 42.6 g

Calcium: 38 mg

Iron: 4.3 mg

Fiber: 4.9 g

Sodium: 437 mg

Cholesterol: 0 mg

■ In large saucepan, melt margarine or butter over medium heat; cook onion and garlic for 3 to 5 minutes or until tender and fragrant but not browned. Stir in curry powder; cook for 1 minute.

■ Stir in lentils, rice and orzo. Add stock; bring to boil. Cover, reduce heat and simmer gently for 35 to 45 minutes or until lentils and rice are tender and liquid is absorbed. Season with salt and pepper to taste. Makes 6 servings.

## COOKING COUSCOUS

■ **In heavy saucepan, bring 2 cups (500 mL) vegetable stock or water to boil; stir in 1-1/4 cups (300 mL) quick-cooking couscous. Remove from heat, cover and let stand for 5 minutes or until tender and liquid is absorbed. Fluff with fork just before serving. Makes about 3 cups (750 mL).**

*Per 1/2-cup (125 mL) Serving: 100 calories, 0.1 g fat, 3.4 g protein, 20.8 g carbohydrate, 7 mg calcium, 0.3 mg iron, 1.1 g fiber, 0 mg sodium, 0 mg cholesterol.*

# Lean and Fast Vegetable Lasagna

**Per Serving:**

Calories: 306

Fat: 6 g

Protein: 16.3 g

Carbohydrate: 49.6 g

Calcium: 422 mg

Iron: 3.5 mg

Fiber: 6.8 g

Sodium: 598 mg

Cholesterol: 15 mg

*This lightened version of lasagna (with no oil or butter in the sauce) is much faster than traditional recipes because it uses timesaving oven-ready noodles.*

| 3 tbsp | all-purpose flour | 50 mL |
|---|---|---|
| 1-1/2 cups | 2% milk | 375 mL |
| 1/2 cup | freshly grated Parmesan cheese | 125 mL |
| 1/4 tsp | nutmeg | 1 mL |
| | Salt and pepper | |
| 4 | carrots | 4 |
| 2 | bunches broccoli (about 1 lb/500 g) | 2 |
| 1 | onion, chopped | 1 |
| 1 cup | sliced mushrooms | 250 mL |
| 1 | can (19 oz/540 mL) tomatoes, drained (reserve juice) | 1 |
| 2 tbsp | tomato paste | 25 mL |
| 1/2 tsp | dried basil | 2 mL |
| 1/4 tsp | dried oregano | 1 mL |
| 6 | oven-ready lasagna noodles | 6 |

■ In small saucepan, blend flour with 1/4 cup (50 mL) of the milk until smooth. Gradually stir in remaining milk. Cook, stirring, over medium heat until thickened. Add half of the cheese, the nutmeg, and salt and pepper to taste. Cook, stirring, for 2 minutes. Place waxed paper directly on surface and set aside.

■ Peel and slice carrots and broccoli stalks; break broccoli florets into bite-size pieces. In saucepan of lightly salted boiling water, cook carrots and broccoli stalks until almost tender-crisp. Add broccoli florets and cook for 3 minutes or until vegetables are tender-crisp; drain well. Gently stir in onion and mushrooms; let stand, covered, for 5 minutes. Stir in cheese sauce; set aside.

■ With potato masher, crush tomatoes in bowl. Stir in tomato paste and enough reserved tomato juice to make 2 cups (500 mL). Stir in basil, oregano, and salt and pepper to taste.

■ Spoon one-third of the tomato mixture into ungreased 8-inch (2 L) square baking dish; arrange half of the noodles over top. Cover with half of the vegetable mixture; spread with half of the remaining tomato mixture. Arrange remaining noodles on top; spoon in remaining vegetables. Cover with remaining tomato mixture; sprinkle with remaining cheese.

■ Cover with foil; bake in 350°F (180°C) oven for 30 to 35 minutes or until sauce is bubbly around edges and noodles are tender. Let stand for 5 minutes. Makes 4 servings.

---

**PERFECT PROTEIN PARTNERS**

Vegetarians know that without meat, poultry, fish and eggs, they must plan a perfect mix of either plant foods or plant foods plus milk products to ensure a complete protein (all the essential amino acids your body cannot make). Here are some vegetarian combinations for a complete protein:

■ peanut butter with whole wheat bread

■ lentils with brown rice

■ split pea soup and whole wheat bread

■ pasta and cheese

■ breakfast cereal with milk

■ nuts plus wheat, oats, corn, rice — e.g., rice pilaf or pasta with nuts

■ tofu plus grains like wheat, corn, rice or rye

## Stuffed Acorn Squash

**Per Serving:**

Calories: 334

Fat: 7.8 g

Protein: 10.2 g

Carbohydrate: 60.3 g

Calcium: 109 mg

Iron: 3.8 mg

Fiber: 11.1 g

Sodium: 445 mg

Cholesterol: 0 mg

*For complete protein, serve this with lentil or bean soup or salad.*

| 1 | acorn squash | 1 |
|---|---|---|
| 2 tsp | margarine or butter | 10 mL |
| 1 | clove garlic, minced | 1 |
| 1 tbsp | minced onion | 15 mL |
| 1 tbsp | minced celery | 15 mL |
| 1/2 cup | bulgur | 125 mL |
| 1 tbsp | chopped raisins | 15 mL |
| 1 tbsp | finely chopped almonds | 15 mL |
| 1/2 tsp | cinnamon | 2 mL |
| 1 cup | chicken or vegetable stock, boiling | 250 mL |
| 1 tbsp | chopped fresh parsley or mint | 15 mL |

■ Halve and seed squash. Bake cut side down on greased baking sheet in 350°F (180°C) oven for 45 to 50 minutes or until tender.

■ Meanwhile, in nonstick saucepan, melt margarine or butter; cook garlic, onion and celery over medium heat for 3 to 5 minutes or until softened. Stir in bulgur, raisins, almonds and cinnamon. Add stock and bring to simmer; reduce heat to low, cover and cook for 15 to 20 minutes or until liquid is absorbed. Spoon into squash. Garnish with parsley. Makes 2 servings.

*Stuffed Acorn Squash*

91

## Pasta with Vegetables and Cheese Sauce

**Per Serving:**

Calories: 610

Fat: 16.3 g

Protein: 30.7 g

Carbohydrate: 84.5 g

Calcium: 643 mg

Iron: 2.5 mg

Fiber: 5.6 g

Sodium: 411 mg

Cholesterol: 50 mg

*We used Canadian Emmenthal in this reduced-fat cheese sauce, but you can use other lightly tangy cheeses such as Fontina, Lappi, Edam or Gouda. Read the label and look for those that have 25 per cent or less milk fat (M.F.).*

| | | |
|---|---|---|
| 3 cups | pasta shells or fusilli | 750 mL |
| 1 | onion | 1 |
| 2 cups | frozen mixed vegetables | 500 mL |
| 1/2 cup | water | 125 mL |
| 2 tbsp | all-purpose flour | 25 mL |
| 1/4 tsp | dry mustard | 1 mL |
| 1/4 tsp | each black pepper, salt and nutmeg | 1 mL |
| Pinch | cayenne pepper | Pinch |
| 1-1/2 cups | 2% milk | 375 mL |
| 1-3/4 cups | shredded Emmenthal cheese (about 6 oz/175 g) | 425 mL |
| 1/4 cup | freshly grated Parmesan cheese | 50 mL |
| 1/4 cup | chopped fresh parsley | 50 mL |

■ In large saucepan of lightly salted boiling water, cook pasta until tender but firm, about 10 minutes.

■ Meanwhile, quarter onion and separate layers. In small heavy saucepan, combine onion, frozen vegetables and water; cover and bring to boil. Reduce heat to medium and cook for 5 minutes. With slotted spoon, transfer vegetables to bowl, leaving cooking liquid in pan. Cover vegetables and keep warm.

■ Blend flour, mustard, black pepper, salt, nutmeg and cayenne into 1/2 cup (125 mL) of the milk until smooth; stir into cooking liquid. Cook, stirring, over medium heat until thickened, 2 to 3 minutes. Stir in remaining milk and Emmenthal and Parmesan cheeses; cook, stirring, until cheese is melted.

■ Drain cooked pasta; return to pan. Stir in vegetables, sauce and parsley; toss and serve. Makes 4 servings.

## Rotini with Olives and Artichokes

*When you don't have any fresh ingredients on hand, a well-stocked larder comes to the rescue with ingredients for this quick and zesty sauce.*

| | | |
|---|---|---|
| 2 tbsp | olive oil | 25 mL |
| 1 cup | black olives, pitted and sliced | 250 mL |
| 1/2 cup | stuffed green olives, sliced | 125 mL |
| 1/3 cup | chopped drained pimientos | 75 mL |
| 1 | jar (6 oz/170 mL) marinated artichokes, drained and sliced | 1 |
| 1 tbsp | chopped capers | 15 mL |
| 4 | cloves garlic, minced | 4 |
| 1 tsp | dried oregano | 5 mL |
| 1/4 tsp | hot pepper flakes | 1 mL |
| 1 | can (14 oz/398 mL) tomatoes (undrained) | 1 |
| 1/4 cup | chopped fresh parsley | 50 mL |
| 3/4 lb | rotini | 375 g |
| 1/2 cup | freshly grated Parmesan cheese | 125 mL |

**Per Serving:**

Calories: 520

Fat: 18 g

Protein: 17.1 g

Carbohydrate: 73.7 g

Calcium: 248 mg

Iron: 3.7 mg

Fiber: 6.3 g

Sodium: 1050 mg

Cholesterol: 8 mg

■ In large skillet, heat oil over medium-high heat; cook black and green olives, pimientos, artichokes, capers, garlic, oregano and hot pepper flakes, stirring frequently, for 3 to 4 minutes or until fragrant.

■ Add tomatoes and mash with potato masher; reduce heat to medium-low and simmer, uncovered, for 10 minutes. Add chopped parsley. Taste and adjust seasoning if necessary.

■ Meanwhile, in large pot of boiling water, cook rotini until tender but firm. Drain well and toss with sauce. Transfer to warmed serving bowl and sprinkle with Parmesan. Makes 4 servings.

## Lentil Chili with Fall Vegetables

**Per Serving:**

Calories: 270

Fat: 6 g

Protein: 15.1 g

Carbohydrate: 43.6 g

Calcium: 69 mg

Iron: 6.5 mg

Fiber: 10.2 g

Sodium: 418 mg

Cholesterol: 0 mg

*A robust-flavored bowl of lentils and vegetables makes a fine supper that's both reheatable and freezeable. Serve with whole wheat toast or rolls, corn bread or fluffy rice.*

**MENU SUGGESTION**

LENTIL CHILI WITH FALL VEGETABLES
*This Page*

CORN BREAD
*Page 39*

WATERMELON SHERBET
*Page 129*

| | | |
|---|---|---|
| 2 tbsp | vegetable oil | 25 mL |
| 1 | large red onion, chopped | 1 |
| 2 | cloves garlic, minced | 2 |
| 2 | zucchini, cubed | 2 |
| 2 | sweet red or yellow peppers, cubed | 2 |
| 1 | large eggplant (unpeeled), cubed | 1 |
| 1 tbsp | chopped fresh hot pepper | 15 mL |
| 4 tsp | chili powder | 20 mL |
| 1 tsp | each cumin, salt and dried oregano | 5 mL |
| 3 cups | chopped tomatoes | 750 mL |
| 2-1/2 cups | vegetable stock | 625 mL |
| 1-1/2 cups | green lentils | 375 mL |
| 2 tbsp | lemon juice | 25 mL |
| | Salt | |

■ In large heavy saucepan, heat oil over medium heat; cook onion and garlic, stirring occasionally, for about 4 minutes or until softened.

■ Add zucchini, sweet peppers, eggplant and hot pepper; cook, stirring occasionally, for 5 minutes. Stir in chili powder, cumin, salt and oregano; cook, stirring, for 5 minutes.

■ Add tomatoes, water and lentils; bring to boil. Reduce heat to medium-low and cook, covered, for 40 to 45 minutes or until thickened and lentils are tender. For thicker chili, uncover and cook, stirring often, to desired consistency. Stir in lemon juice, and salt to taste. Makes 6 servings.

## Couscous Pilaf

*Middle Eastern comfort food, couscous (a pre-cooked grain) is one of the fastest dishes to prepare.*

**Per Serving:**

Calories: 237

Fat: 6.5 g

Protein: 8.6 g

Carbohydrate: 37 g

Calcium: 50 mg

Iron: 1.4 mg

Fiber: 2.7 g

Sodium: 344 mg

Cholesterol: 0 mg

| | | |
|---|---|---|
| 1 tsp | vegetable oil | 5 mL |
| 1 | onion, finely chopped | 1 |
| 1 | clove garlic, minced | 1 |
| 1/2 tsp | ground cumin | 2 mL |
| 1/4 tsp | ground coriander | 1 mL |
| 1/4 tsp | ground ginger | 1 mL |
| 1-3/4 cups | chicken or vegetable stock | 425 mL |
| 1 cup | quick-cooking couscous | 250 mL |
| 1/4 cup | raisins | 50 mL |
| 2 tbsp | chopped fresh parsley or coriander | 25 mL |
| | Salt and pepper | |
| 1/4 cup | chopped toasted almonds | 50 mL |

■ In heavy saucepan, heat oil over medium-low heat; cook onion and garlic, stirring, for 2 to 3 minutes or until onion is softened. Add cumin, coriander and ginger; cook, stirring, for 1 minute or until aromatic. Add stock and bring to simmer.

■ Remove from heat; stir in couscous and raisins. Cover and let stand for 5 minutes; fluff with a fork. Stir in parsley; season with salt and pepper to taste. Transfer to serving dish; sprinkle with almonds. Makes 4 servings.

# Satisfying Salads and Side Dishes

**S**alads and vegetables are an easy and colorful way to make main dishes tastier and more nutritious. We've included recipes like Green Bean and Red Pepper Salad and Parsnip and Carrots with Almonds that make the most of vegetables and greens in season. And we've added appetizing main-dish salads that are chock-full of meat or fish, vegetables and pasta or grains. Enjoy them any time of year for a light and satisfying lunch or dinner.

## Brown Rice and Salmon Salad Plate

**Per Serving:**

Calories: 361

Fat: 13 g

Protein: 15.8 g

Carbohydrate: 44.7 g

Calcium: 198 mg

Iron: 2.4 mg

Fiber: 2.6 g

Sodium: 782 mg

Cholesterol: 19 mg

*Grains, fish and crunchy vegetables are tastily combined in this nutritious main-course salad. You can substitute pink salmon or water-packed tuna for the red salmon. Both are lower in fat. Serve with pumpernickel toast, cheese and fresh fruit.*

| 1 cup | brown rice | 250 mL |
|---|---|---|
| 2 | stalks celery, diced | 2 |
| Half | seedless cucumber, diced | Half |
| 3 | green onions, chopped | 3 |
| 1/4 cup | chopped fresh dill | 50 mL |
| 1 | can (7-1/2 oz/213 g) red salmon, drained | 1 |
| | Lettuce leaves | |
| | Fresh dill sprigs | |

**Dressing:**

| 1 tbsp | lemon juice | 15 mL |
|---|---|---|
| 1 tsp | grated lemon rind | 5 mL |
| 2 tsp | Dijon mustard | 10 mL |
| Pinch | each salt and pepper | Pinch |
| 2 tbsp | vegetable oil | 25 mL |

■ In large pot of boiling salted water, cook rice for 25 to 30 minutes or just until tender. Drain and refresh under cold running water; drain again and set aside.

**Dressing:** In large bowl, whisk together lemon juice and rind, mustard, salt and pepper; gradually whisk in oil.

■ Add cooked rice, celery, cucumber, green onions and chopped dill; toss to mix well.

■ Remove skin and bones from salmon; break into bite-size chunks. Add to salad and toss gently. *(Salad can be covered and refrigerated for up to 1 day.)*

■ Line 4 plates with lettuce leaves. Spoon salad over top and garnish with dill sprigs. Makes 4 servings.

> **BROWN RICE**
>
> Brown rice is getting rave reviews these days! Along with other whole grains and breads, it is a complex carbohydrate that adds vital nutrients and fiber to dishes — along with great taste and texture. Serve it with fish, meat or poultry or add it to salads or meatless dishes for a nutritious meal.

*Brown Rice and Salmon Salad Plate*

## Rutabaga au Gratin

**Per Serving:**

Calories: 98

Fat: 1.1 g

Protein: 2.1 g

Carbohydrate: 21.8 g

Calcium: 58 mg

Iron: 1 mg

Fiber: 2.8 g

Sodium: 44 mg

Cholesterol: 3 mg

*A little light cream cheese adds just a touch of richness to the sauce in this flavorful vegetable dish. Serve it with a favorite roast.*

| | | |
|---|---|---|
| 1 | rutabaga (about 1 lb/500 g) | 1 |
| 1 | onion, thinly sliced | 1 |
| 1 cup | apple cider or juice | 250 mL |
| 4 tsp | all-purpose flour | 20 mL |
| Pinch | nutmeg | Pinch |
| 1 tbsp | light cream cheese | 15 mL |
| | Salt and pepper | |
| 2 tbsp | fresh whole wheat bread crumbs | 25 mL |
| 1 tsp | packed brown sugar | 5 mL |

■ Peel and thinly slice rutabaga. In large saucepan of lightly salted boiling water, cook rutabaga for 10 minutes; add onion and cook for 5 minutes or just until tender. Drain and place in shallow 6- or 8-cup (1.5 or 2 L) baking dish.

■ In saucepan, whisk together cider, flour and nutmeg. Bring to boil over medium-high heat; cook, whisking for 1 minute or until thickened. Whisk in cream cheese until melted. Season with salt and pepper to taste. Pour over rutabaga mixture.

■ Combine crumbs with brown sugar; sprinkle over rutabaga mixture. Bake in 350°F (180°C) oven for 20 to 25 minutes or until top is golden. Makes 4 servings.

*Warm Acorn Squash and Apple Salad*

**MENU SUGGESTION**

BROCCOLI-STUFFED TURKEY LOAF
*Page 60*

WARM ACORN SQUASH
AND APPLE SALAD
*This Page*

CRANBERRY CRUMBLE DESSERT
*Page 124*

# Warm Acorn Squash and Apple Salad

**Per Serving:**

Calories: 273

Fat: 16.6 g

Protein: 2.7 g

Carbohydrate: 33.6 g

Calcium: 61 mg

Iron: 1.5 mg

Fiber: 6.5 g

Sodium: 187 mg

Cholesterol: 0 mg

*In this delicious warm salad, tender sweet squash and crisp red apples such as Cortland or McIntosh provide exciting contrasts in taste and texture.*

| | | |
|---|---|---|
| 1 | acorn squash | 1 |
| 2 | apples (unpeeled) | 2 |
| 1/2 cup | finely chopped red onion | 125 mL |
| | Lettuce leaves | |
| 1/2 cup | chopped pecans | 125 mL |

**Dressing:**

| | | |
|---|---|---|
| 2 tbsp | cider vinegar | 25 mL |
| 2 tbsp | apple juice | 25 mL |
| 1 tbsp | liquid honey | 15 mL |
| 1 tbsp | Dijon mustard | 15 mL |
| 1/4 tsp | salt | 1 mL |
| Pinch | pepper | Pinch |
| 2 tbsp | vegetable oil | 25 mL |

**Dressing:** In large bowl, whisk together vinegar, apple juice, honey, mustard, salt and pepper. Gradually whisk in oil; set aside.

■ Cut squash into 6 or 8 pieces; remove seeds. Place in steamer; cover and steam for 5 to 8 minutes or just until tender. Drain; remove skin. Cut squash into 1-inch (2.5 cm) cubes; add to bowl and toss gently with dressing.

■ Dice apples and add to squash mixture along with onion; toss to mix. Arrange on lettuce leaves; top with pecans and serve immediately. Makes 4 servings.

# Potato and Turnip Gratin

*Simple and comforting, this vegetable gratin is elegant enough to grace any table.*

| | | |
|---|---|---|
| 1 | leek (white part only), finely chopped | 1 |
| 1 | large onion, finely chopped | 1 |
| 1 | small white turnip, peeled and finely sliced | 1 |
| 1 lb | potatoes, peeled and finely sliced (about 4 medium) | 500 g |
| 1/2 tsp | salt | 2 mL |
| Pinch | pepper | Pinch |
| 1/2 cup | chicken stock | 125 mL |
| 1 tsp | chopped fresh parsley | 5 mL |

**Per Serving:**

Calories: 126

Fat: 0.4 g

Protein: 3.3 g

Carbohydrate: 28.6 g

Calcium: 37 mg

Iron: 0.9 mg

Fiber: 3.3 g

Sodium: 431 mg

Cholesterol: 0 mg

■ In large bowl, toss together leek, onion, turnip, potatoes, salt and pepper. Transfer to shallow 6-cup (1.5 L) casserole dish, pressing mixture down firmly.

■ Pour chicken stock over vegetables; cover and bake in 300°F (150°C) oven for 1 hour. Uncover and bake for 30 to 45 minutes longer or until vegetables are tender. Sprinkle with parsley. Makes 4 servings.

**SPICE IT UP!**
**Fresh and dried herbs and spices add flavor and variety to foods — without adding calories or sodium. Try seasoning salads and vegetables with tarragon, cumin, basil, thyme or oregano. Remember the rule of thumb is three times as much fresh herbs as dried. Add a pinch of nutmeg and cinnamon to fruit desserts, or a bit of saffron or curry to rice or other grain dishes.**

## Creamy Buttermilk Dressing

**Per Tbsp (15 mL):**

Calories: 19

Fat: 1.6 g

Protein: 0.3 g

Carbohydrate: 0.8 g

Calcium: 10 mg

Iron: 0 mg

Fiber: 0 g

Sodium: 57 mg

Cholesterol: 3 mg

*Extend this dressing to make a sauce. For fish, add 1/4 cup (50 mL) finely chopped cucumber to 1 cup (250 mL) dressing. For lamb, add 1 clove garlic, minced, and 2 tsp (10 mL) finely chopped fresh mint, as well as the cucumber.*

| 3/4 cup | buttermilk | 175 mL |
|---|---|---|
| 1/2 cup | light mayonnaise | 125 mL |
| 2 tsp | Dijon mustard | 10 mL |
| Dash | lemon juice | Dash |
| 1 tsp | crushed green peppercorns | 5 mL |
| 2 tbsp | chopped chives | 15 mL |
| | Salt | |

■ In bowl, whisk together buttermilk, mayonnaise, mustard, lemon juice and peppercorns; stir in chives. Cover and refrigerate for 30 minutes. Season with salt to taste. Makes 1-1/2 cups (375 mL).

## Oriental Vinaigrette

**Per Tbsp (15 mL):**

Calories: 18

Fat: 1.3 g

Protein: 0.2 g

Carbohydrate: 1.7 g

Calcium: 2 mg

Iron: 0.1 mg

Fiber: 0 g

Sodium: 117 mg

Cholesterol: 0 mg

*Rice vinegar is available in many supermarkets. Its mildness is particularly suited for dressings low in oil. This dressing goes well with raw or cooked vegetable salads.*

| 1/3 cup | rice vinegar | 75 mL |
|---|---|---|
| 4 tsp | soy sauce | 20 mL |
| 2 tsp | Dijon mustard | 10 mL |
| 2 tsp | liquid honey | 10 mL |
| Pinch | grated gingerroot | Pinch |
| Dash | hot pepper sauce | Dash |
| 2 tsp | sesame oil | 10 mL |
| 1 tsp | vegetable oil | 5 mL |

■ In small bowl, whisk together vinegar, soy sauce, mustard, honey, gingerroot and hot pepper sauce; whisk in sesame and vegetable oils. Makes 2/3 cup (150 mL).

## Herbed Yogurt Vinaigrette

*This full-flavored creamy dressing is good on almost any green or mixed vegetable salad but especially on cucumber or potato salad.*

| 2 tbsp | white wine vinegar | 25 mL |
|---|---|---|
| 2 tbsp | lemon juice | 25 mL |
| 1 | clove garlic, crushed | 1 |
| 1 tsp | granulated sugar | 5 mL |
| 1/2 tsp | Dijon mustard | 2 mL |
| 1 tsp | chopped fresh dill (or 1/2 tsp/2 mL dried dillweed) | 5 mL |
| 1/2 tsp | each chopped fresh tarragon and marjoram (or 1/4 tsp/1 mL each dried) | 2 mL |
| 2 tbsp | vegetable oil | 25 mL |
| 3/4 cup | low-fat yogurt | 175 mL |
| | Salt and pepper | |

**Per Tbsp (15 mL):**

Calories: 25

Fat: 1.9 g

Protein: 0.6 g

Carbohydrate: 1.4 g

Calcium: 23 mg

Iron: 0.1 mg

Fiber: 0 g

Sodium: 8 mg

Cholesterol: 1 mg

■ In small bowl, whisk together vinegar, lemon juice, garlic, sugar, mustard, dill, tarragon and marjoram; whisk in oil and yogurt. Season with salt and pepper to taste. Cover and chill. Makes 1 cup (250 mL).

---

**NOT ALL GREENS ARE CREATED EQUAL**

Iceberg lettuce may be what you grew up with but if you want to get the most out of the greens in your salads, remember that darker colored greens generally contain more vitamins and minerals like betacarotene and calcium. To improve the nutritional value of salad, mix various greens together. Excellent choices are escarole, chicory, raw spinach, Swiss chard, Boston lettuce, watercress and arugula.

## Green Bean Salad with Niçoise Vinaigrette

**Per Serving:**

Calories: 163

Fat: 7.3 g

Protein: 5.2 g

Carbohydrate: 20.8 g

Calcium: 53 mg

Iron: 1.8 mg

Fiber: 3.4 g

Sodium: 114 mg

Cholesterol: 72 mg

*If you've ever wished for more green beans in your salade niçoise, you'll enjoy this version, which dispenses with the tuna and doubles up on tender young beans. Soaking the onion in water before adding it to the salad gives it a milder flavor.*

| | | |
|---|---|---|
| 1/2 cup | thinly sliced red onion | 125 mL |
| 1 lb | new potatoes (unpeeled) | 500 g |
| 1 lb | green beans, trimmed | 500 g |
| 2 | hard-cooked eggs | 2 |
| 1/4 cup | pitted black olives | 50 mL |

**Vinaigrette:**

| | | |
|---|---|---|
| 1 tbsp | white wine vinegar | 15 mL |
| 1 tbsp | balsamic vinegar | 15 mL |
| 2 | garlic cloves, minced | 2 |
| 1 tbsp | Dijon mustard | 15 mL |
| 1 tsp | anchovy paste | 5 mL |
| Pinch | pepper | Pinch |
| 2 tbsp | olive oil | 25 mL |

**Vinaigrette:** Whisk together wine and balsamic vinegars, garlic, mustard, anchovy paste and pepper; gradually whisk in oil. Set aside.

■ In bowl, cover onion with cold water; let stand for 30 minutes. Drain and set aside.

■ Meanwhile, scrub potatoes and cook in boiling water for 15 to 18 minutes or just until tender. Drain and slice into large bowl. Toss with half of the vinaigrette; set aside.

■ In saucepan of boiling water, cook beans for 5 to 8 minutes or until tender-crisp. Drain and refresh under cold water; pat dry. Add to potatoes along with onion and remaining vinaigrette; toss well.

■ Cut eggs into wedges; arrange along with olives over salad. Makes 6 servings.

*Green Bean Salad with Niçoise Vinaigrette*

## Beet and Spinach Salad

**Per Serving:**

Calories: 110

Fat: 4.1 g

Protein: 4.7 g

Carbohydrate: 15 g

Calcium: 129 mg

Iron: 2.4 mg

Fiber: 4.6 g

Sodium: 131 mg

Cholesterol: 2 mg

*Cook and peel beets, wash and dry lettuce, and mix dressing ahead of time. Assemble salad at serving time. It goes well with grilled fish steaks, chicken breasts or lamb chops.*

| 1-1/2 lb | beets, trimmed | 750 g |
|---|---|---|
| 4 cups | loosely packed torn spinach leaves | 1 L |
| 1 | green onion, chopped | 1 |

**Dressing:**

| 1/2 cup | low-fat yogurt | 125 mL |
|---|---|---|
| 1 tbsp | lemon juice | 15 mL |
| 1 tbsp | vegetable oil | 15 mL |
| 1 tsp | prepared horseradish | 5 mL |
| 1 tsp | liquid honey | 5 mL |
| Half | small clove garlic, minced | Half |

■ In saucepan of boiling water, cook beets for 30 to 45 minutes or until tender. (Alternatively, in 8-cup/2 L microwaveable casserole, combine beets with 1/2 cup/125 mL water. Cover and microwave at High for 15 to 20 minutes or until tender, turning beets over halfway through.) Drain and let cool. Slip off skins; slice and refrigerate until chilled.

**Dressing:** Whisk together yogurt, lemon juice, oil, horseradish, honey and garlic.

■ Arrange bed of spinach on each of 4 plates; arrange chilled beets on top. Drizzle half of the dressing over salad; sprinkle with green onion. Pass remaining dressing. Makes 4 servings.

*Beet and Spinach Salad with grilled fish steaks and potatoes*

## Fresh Tomato Salsa

*Salsa in Spanish simply means sauce, but it has none of the cream and butter that make some sauces too rich for everyday eating. Add the fresh flavor of salsa to burgers, grilled chicken, fish or chops, tacos and omelettes.*

| 1-1/2 cups | diced seeded peeled tomatoes | 375 mL |
|---|---|---|
| 1/4 cup | chopped red onion | 50 mL |
| 1/4 cup | chopped sweet yellow pepper | 50 mL |
| 2 tbsp | chopped celery | 25 mL |
| 2 tbsp | olive oil | 25 mL |
| 1 tbsp | red wine vinegar or cider vinegar | 15 mL |
| 1-1/2 tsp | (approx) minced fresh hot pepper | 7 mL |
| 1/4 cup | chopped fresh coriander or parsley | 50 mL |
| | Salt and pepper | |

■ In bowl, combine tomatoes, onion, yellow pepper, celery, oil, vinegar and hot pepper; cover and let stand for about 20 minutes for flavors to blend. Stir in coriander; season with salt and pepper to taste, and more hot pepper if desired. Makes 2 cups (500 mL).

**Per Tbsp (15 mL):**

Calories: 10

Fat: 0.9 g

Protein: 0.1 g

Carbohydrate: 0.6 g

Calcium: 2 mg

Iron: 0.1 mg

Fiber: 0.2 g

Sodium: 1 mg

Cholesterol: 0 mg

**VEGETABLE VALUE**

To get the most nutrition out of garden-fresh vegetables:

■ eat vegetables raw and unpeeled whenever possible.

■ leave vegetables whole or cut into large chunks. Vitamins and minerals are lost once cut surfaces are exposed to light, air and heat.

■ don't soak vegetables or cook them in too much water; you'll lose valuable water-soluble B vitamins and vitamin C.

■ add the water from cooked vegetables to sauces, soups and stews.

■ cook vegetables with skins on — and cook for the shortest time possible to preserve nutrients.

## Light Coleslaw

**Per Serving:**

Calories: 86

Fat: 4.9 g

Protein: 1.3 g

Carbohydrate: 10.8 g

Calcium: 43 mg

Iron: 0.8 mg

Fiber: 2.2 g

Sodium: 49 mg

Cholesterol: 0 mg

*Light in calories and fresh-tasting, this coleslaw is a natural with any main-course dish or for packed lunches. Use red or green, plain or savoy cabbage.*

| | | |
|---|---|---|
| 4 cups | finely sliced green cabbage | 1 L |
| 2 | small carrots, coarsely grated | 2 |
| 2 | stalks celery, julienned | 2 |
| Half | sweet green pepper, julienned | Half |
| Half | small red apple (unpeeled), julienned | Half |
| 3 | green onions (white and pale green parts), julienned | 3 |

**Dressing:**

| | | |
|---|---|---|
| 2 tbsp | apple juice | 25 mL |
| 1 tbsp | cider vinegar | 15 mL |
| 2 tsp | Dijon mustard | 10 mL |
| 2 tsp | liquid honey | 10 mL |
| 2 tbsp | vegetable oil | 25 mL |
| 1 tbsp | finely chopped fresh parsley | 15 mL |
| | Salt and pepper | |

**Dressing:** In large bowl, whisk together apple juice, vinegar, mustard and honey; gradually whisk in oil. Stir in parsley; season with salt and pepper to taste.

■ Add cabbage and carrots; toss to mix. Add celery, green pepper, apple and green onions; toss well. Makes 6 servings.

**Light Corn Slaw: Use half green and half red cabbage. Instead of slivered carrots, use drained whole canned baby corn cobs. Substitute julienned large gherkins for celery. Add 1 tbsp (15 mL) chopped fresh dill to dressing.**

**Light Pepper Slaw: Omit apple and add colorful assortment (about 1 cup/250 mL) of sweet peppers. Add a little grated orange rind to dressing.**

## Winter Vegetable Salad

*Serve this delicious salad warm or cold. Cut the root vegetables about the thickness of French fries and cook on top of the stove or microwave all in one pot.*

| | | |
|---|---|---|
| 2 | carrots, cut in sticks | 2 |
| Half | small rutabaga, cut in sticks | Half |
| 1 | baking potato | 1 |
| 1 tbsp | toasted sesame seeds* | 15 mL |
| 1 cup | thinly sliced celery | 250 mL |
| 3 | green onions, chopped | 3 |
| | Salt and pepper | |

**Dressing:**

| | | |
|---|---|---|
| 2 tbsp | white wine vinegar | 25 mL |
| 1 tsp | granulated sugar | 5 mL |
| 1 tsp | Dijon mustard | 5 mL |
| 2 tbsp | olive oil | 25 mL |
| | Salt and pepper | |

**Per Serving:**

Calories: 113

Fat: 5.5 g

Protein: 2.1 g

Carbohydrate: 15.4 g

Calcium: 44 mg

Iron: 1.1 mg

Fiber: 2.7 g

Sodium: 44 mg

Cholesterol: 0 mg

**Dressing:** In serving bowl, whisk together vinegar, sugar and mustard; gradually whisk in oil. Season with salt and pepper to taste; set aside.

■ In saucepan of boiling water, cook carrots and rutabaga for 4 to 5 minutes or until partly cooked. Meanwhile, cut potato into 1-1/2 × 1/2-inch (4 × 1 cm) sticks; add to pan and cook until vegetables are tender-crisp. Drain well. (Alternatively, in microwaveable bowl, combine carrots, rutabaga, potato and 1 cup/250 mL water; cover and microwave at High for 8 minutes or until tender-crisp, stirring occasionally. Drain well.)

■ Toss cooked vegetables with dressing and sesame seeds. Add celery and onions; toss again. Season with salt and pepper to taste. Makes 6 servings.

*Toast sesame seeds in small skillet over low heat, shaking pan, until fragrant and lightly browned, about 5 minutes.

# Chutney Rice Salad

**Per Serving:**

Calories: 245

Fat: 9 g

Protein: 3.7 g

Carbohydrate: 39.7 g

Calcium: 38 mg

Iron: 1.1 mg

Fiber: 3.2 g

Sodium: 347 mg

Cholesterol: 0 mg

*Serve this salad spooned into individual custard cups or on a bed of shredded lettuce.*

| | | |
|---|---|---|
| 3 cups | cooked brown rice, chilled (3/4 cup/175 mL raw) | 750 mL |
| 1-1/4 cups | finely chopped (unpeeled) Granny Smith apples | 300 mL |
| 1 cup | thinly sliced celery | 250 mL |
| 1/2 cup | golden raisins | 125 mL |
| 1/2 cup | mango chutney | 125 mL |
| 2 tbsp | toasted slivered almonds* | 25 mL |
| 3 tbsp | vegetable oil | 45 mL |

■ In bowl, combine rice, apples, celery, raisins, chutney and almonds. Add oil and mix well. Refrigerate until chilled. Makes 6 servings.

*To toast almonds, bake on baking sheet in 350°F (180°C) oven for 10 minutes or until golden.

*Chutney Rice Salad*

# Spring Lamb Salad

Spring Lamb
Salad

| Per Serving: | | |
|---|---|---|
| Calories: 261 | | |

*Lamb, watercress and fresh mint are a winning combination in this light and easy salad.*

| | | |
|---|---|---|
| Fat: 12.2 g | 1 | small head romaine or Bibb lettuce | 1 |

| | | | |
|---|---|---|---|
| 1 | small head romaine or Bibb lettuce | 1 |
| 1 | small bunch watercress | 1 |
| 1 | small sweet red pepper, cut in strips | 1 |

**Per Serving:**

Calories: 261

Fat: 12.2 g

Protein: 24.6 g

Carbohydrate: 13.4 g

Calcium: 88 mg

Iron: 3.4 mg

Fiber: 3.8 g

Sodium: 100 mg

Cholesterol: 71 mg

**Topping:**

| | | |
|---|---|---|
| 2 tbsp | vegetable oil | 25 mL |
| 1 lb | boneless lean lamb, cut in thin strips | 500 g |
| 1 | onion, chopped | 1 |
| 1 cup | frozen peas | 250 mL |
| 1 tbsp | chopped fresh mint | 15 mL |
| 1 tbsp | mint jelly | 15 mL |
| 1 tbsp | lemon juice | 15 mL |
| 1 tbsp | apple cider vinegar | 15 mL |
| | Salt and pepper | |

■ Tear lettuce into bite-size pieces; remove stems from watercress. In salad bowl, combine lettuce, watercress and red pepper.

**Topping:** In heavy skillet, heat 1 tbsp (15 mL) of the oil over medium-high heat until sizzling; cook lamb, stirring constantly, for about 3 minutes or until no longer pink. Remove lamb and set aside.

■ In same skillet, cook onion for about 3 minutes or until softened. Stir in remaining oil, peas, mint and jelly, lemon juice, vinegar, and salt and pepper to taste. Bring to boil over medium heat, stirring occasionally. Return lamb to skillet; cook for about 1 minute or until heated through. Pour over salad and toss gently. Serve immediately. Makes 4 servings.

## Carrot Custard Moulds

**Per Serving:**

Calories: 85

Fat: 4.2 g

Protein: 3.1 g

Carbohydrate: 8.8 g

Calcium: 47 mg

Iron: 0.6 mg

Fiber: 1.3 g

Sodium: 124 mg

Cholesterol: 55 mg

*These little moulds are delicious hot and just as good cold. For a unique salad, unmould each chilled one on shredded lettuce and garnish with drizzled yogurt or chopped sweet pickle.*

| 1-1/2 cups | sliced carrots | 375 mL |
|---|---|---|
| 2 tbsp | minced onion | 25 mL |
| 2 tsp | margarine or butter | 10 mL |
| 6 | soda crackers | 6 |
| 1/3 cup | 2% milk | 75 mL |
| 1 | egg | 1 |
| Pinch | white pepper | Pinch |
| 1/4 cup | low-fat yogurt (optional) | 50 mL |

■ In saucepan of boiling water, cook carrots and onion until carrots are tender; drain well and stir in margarine or butter to coat.

■ In food processor, process crackers until fine; add carrot mixture and milk. Process for 1 minute or until puréed. Add egg and pepper; process for 30 seconds or until smooth.

■ Divide mixture among 4 lightly greased 3/4-cup (175 mL) custard cups; arrange in large baking dish. Pour in enough boiling water to come halfway up sides of cups. Bake in 350°F (180°C) oven for about 35 minutes or until firm to the touch. Unmould and serve immediately with yogurt (if using). Makes 4 servings.

### Microwave method:

■ In microwaveable dish, combine carrots, onion, margarine or butter and 1/4 cup (50 mL) water; cover and microwave at High for 5 minutes or until carrots are tender.

■ In food processor, process crackers until fine; add carrot mixture and milk. Process for 1 minute or until puréed. Add egg and pepper; process for 30 seconds or until smooth.

■ Divide mixture among 4 lightly greased 3/4-cup (175 mL) custard cups. Cover with vented plastic wrap. Microwave at High for 5 minutes, rearranging once. Let stand for 3 minutes. Unmould and serve immediately with yogurt (if using). Makes 4 servings.

## Peas and Green Onions

*This easy vegetable dish is a tasty accompaniment to chicken or fish. If desired, line the serving bowl with fresh lettuce leaves before adding the onions and peas.*

| 2 lb | fresh unshelled peas | 1 kg |
|---|---|---|
| 6 | green onions (white parts only) | 6 |
| 1/4 cup | water | 50 mL |
| 4 | large leaf or Boston lettuce leaves | 4 |
| 2 tsp | margarine or butter | 10 mL |
| Pinch | granulated sugar | Pinch |
| | Salt and pepper | |

■ Shell peas, reserving several pods. Cut onions into 1-inch (2.5 cm) lengths. Pour water into 8-cup (2 L) saucepan; line pan with lettuce. Place peas, reserved pods, onions, margarine or butter and sugar in leaves; cover and bring just to boil. Reduce heat to medium-low and cook for 7 to 8 minutes or until peas are tender. Drain; discard pea pods. Season with salt and pepper to taste. Discard lettuce. Makes 4 servings.

**Per Serving:**

Calories: 88

Fat: 2.1 g

Protein: 4.6 g

Carbohydrate: 13.3 g

Calcium: 28 mg

Iron: 1.4 mg

Fiber: 5.7 g

Sodium: 25 mg

Cholesterol: 0 mg

> **HURRAY FOR VITAMIN A!**
> Carrots — as well as other dark yellow, red, and leafy green vegetables such as broccoli and spinach — contain large amounts of betacarotene, a form of vitamin A. In fact, 1/2 cup (125 mL) cooked carrots contains almost twice the daily requirement of vitamin A for an adult.

# Light Caesar Salad

**Per Serving:**

Calories: 109

Fat: 6.4 g

Protein: 4 g

Carbohydrate: 9.9 g

Calcium: 92 mg

Iron: 1.5 mg

Fiber: 2.2 g

Sodium: 237 mg

Cholesterol: 3 mg

*The dressing for this salad is almost as creamy as the old-fashioned egg yolk version and just as piquant. It clings as it should if you make sure the lettuce is thoroughly drained and dried after washing.*

| 2 | slices whole wheat bread, cubed | 2 |
|---|---|---|
| 2 tbsp | white wine vinegar | 25 mL |
| 1 tbsp | Dijon mustard | 15 mL |
| 1 | large clove garlic, minced | 1 |
| 1/2 tsp | lemon juice | 2 mL |
| | Worcestershire sauce | |
| 1/4 cup | freshly grated Parmesan cheese | 50 mL |
| 1/4 cup | light mayonnaise | 50 mL |
| 1 tbsp | water | 15 mL |
| 1 tbsp | olive oil | 15 mL |
| | Salt and pepper | |
| 2 tbsp | fresh bread crumbs | 25 mL |
| 1 | large head romaine lettuce | 1 |

■ In lightly greased cake pan or pie plate, bake bread cubes in 350°F (180°C) oven for 10 to 12 minutes or until golden, turning halfway through; set aside.

■ In salad bowl, whisk together vinegar, mustard, garlic, lemon juice, and Worcestershire sauce to taste. Whisk in Parmesan cheese, then mayonnaise. Gradually whisk in water, then oil. Season with salt and pepper to taste. Stir in bread crumbs.

■ Tear lettuce into bite-size pieces; toss with dressing. Add croutons and toss again. Makes 6 servings.

# Green Bean and Red Pepper Salad

*For an easy summer meal, serve this colorful salad with slices of cold chicken or turkey breast. Add a refreshing frozen fruit yogurt for dessert.*

**Per Serving:**

Calories: 111

Fat: 9.3 g

Protein: 1.6 g

Carbohydrate: 6.9 g

Calcium: 34 mg

Iron: 1.1 mg

Fiber: 2.4 g

Sodium: 243 mg

Cholesterol: 0 mg

| 1 lb | green beans, trimmed | 500 g |
|---|---|---|
| 1 | sweet red pepper, chopped | 1 |

**Dressing:**

| 2 tbsp | lemon juice | 25 mL |
|---|---|---|
| 1 tbsp | Dijon mustard | 15 mL |
| 1 tsp | dried oregano | 5 mL |
| 1/2 tsp | granulated sugar | 2 mL |
| 1/2 tsp | each salt and pepper | 2 mL |
| 1 | clove garlic, minced (optional) | 1 |
| 1/4 cup | olive oil | 50 mL |

■ Cut beans in half lengthwise if beans are thick. In saucepan of lightly salted boiling water, cook beans for 10 to 12 minutes or until tender-crisp. (Alternatively, place beans in 8-cup (2 L) microwaveable casserole. Add 1/4 cup (50 mL) water; cover and microwave at High for 7 to 10 minutes or until tender-crisp, stirring twice.) Drain and refresh under cold running water; drain again and pat dry. Place in salad bowl and toss with red pepper.

**Dressing:** In small bowl, combine lemon juice, mustard, oregano, sugar, salt, pepper, and garlic (if using); whisk in oil. Pour over bean mixture and toss. Taste and adjust seasoning if necessary.

Makes 6 servings.

## Spinach, Watercress and Apple Salad with Cranberry Dressing

**Per Serving:**

Calories: 109

Fat: 7.1 g

Protein: 2.1 g

Carbohydrate: 11.1 g

Calcium: 80 mg

Iron: 1.4 mg

Fiber: 1.9 g

Sodium: 110 mg

Cholesterol: 0 mg

*For variety, you can use any lettuce for this salad and add a sliced pear, or grapefruit or orange sections. The dressing can be prepared a few days ahead, and early in the day, the greens can be washed, wrapped in towels and refrigerated in plastic bags.*

| | | |
|---|---|---|
| **6 cups** | **torn spinach** | **1.5 L** |
| **4 cups** | **watercress** | **1 L** |
| **4 cups** | **torn Boston lettuce** | **1 L** |
| **1 tbsp** | **lemon juice** | **15 mL** |
| **1** | **firm red apple** | **1** |

**Cranberry Dressing:**

| | | |
|---|---|---|
| 1/3 cup | concentrated cranberry cocktail | 75 mL |
| 1/4 cup | vegetable oil | 50 mL |
| 2 tbsp | rice vinegar or wine vinegar | 25 mL |
| 1/4 tsp | salt | 1 mL |
| Pinch | each dry mustard, granulated sugar and pepper | Pinch |

**Cranberry Dressing:** In small bowl, whisk together cranberry cocktail, oil, vinegar, salt, mustard, sugar and pepper.

■ In large salad bowl, toss together spinach, watercress and lettuce. In small bowl, mix lemon juice with 2 tbsp (25 mL) water. Core and slice apple into thin wedges; add to lemon juice mixture and toss to coat.

■ Scatter over salad. Pour dressing over salad; toss to mix. Makes 8 servings.

*Spinach, Watercress and Apple Salad with Cranberry Dressing*

## Parsnip and Carrots with Almonds

**Per Serving:**

Calories: 200

Fat: 6.5 g

Protein: 3.3 g

Carbohydrate: 35 g

Calcium: 81 mg

Iron: 1.6 mg

Fiber: 6.2 g

Sodium: 98 mg

Cholesterol: 0 mg

*This makes a colorful vegetable dish with a crunchy topping. Easily doubled, it can be prepared a day or two in advance. Reheat in 325°F (160°C) oven for 25 to 30 minutes or until heated through. Top with parsley and nuts just before serving.*

| | | |
|---|---|---|
| 2 tbsp | sliced almonds | 25 mL |
| 2 cups | sliced peeled parsnips (about 3/4 lb/375 g) | 500 mL |
| 2 cups | sliced peeled carrots (about 3/4 lb/375 g) | 500 mL |
| 2 tbsp | packed brown sugar | 25 mL |
| 2 tbsp | apple or orange juice | 25 mL |
| 1 tbsp | margarine or butter | 15 mL |
| Pinch | nutmeg | Pinch |
| | Salt and pepper | |
| 1 tbsp | minced fresh parsley | 15 mL |

■ On baking sheet, toast almonds in 350°F (180°C) oven for 5 minutes or until lightly browned; set aside.

■ In saucepan of boiling water, cook parsnips and carrots for about 15 minutes or until tender; drain well.

■ In food processor or using potato masher, mash vegetables thoroughly. Stir in sugar, apple juice, margarine or butter, nutmeg, and salt and pepper to taste; spoon into casserole. Sprinkle or attractively arrange almonds over top. Sprinkle with parsley. Makes 4 servings.

*Parsnip and Carrots with Almonds*

## Braised Squash

**Per Serving:**

Calories: 141

Fat: 4.2 g

Protein: 2.9 g

Carbohydrate: 26.9 g

Calcium: 113 mg

Iron: 1.9 mg

Fiber: 0.5 g

Sodium: 122 mg

Cholesterol: 0 mg

*Choose any easy-to-peel fleshy squash, such as butternut, for this harvest side dish.*

| | | |
|---|---|---|
| 2 tbsp | olive oil | 25 mL |
| 1 | large onion, chopped | 1 |
| 3 | cloves garlic, minced | 3 |
| 8 cups | cubed peeled squash (about 3-1/2 lb/1.75 kg) | 2 L |
| 1/2 tsp | dried thyme or oregano | 2 mL |
| 1/2 cup | chicken stock or dry white wine | 125 mL |
| 1/4 cup | chopped fresh parsley or green onion | 50 mL |
| | Salt and pepper | |

■ In large heavy saucepan, heat oil over medium-low heat; cook onion and garlic until softened, about 4 minutes. Add squash and thyme, mixing well; cook, stirring occasionally, for 2 minutes.

■ Pour in stock; reduce heat to simmer and cook, covered and gently stirring occasionally, for 12 minutes. Uncover and cook for about 5 minutes longer or until squash is tender and most of the stock has been absorbed. *(Recipe can be prepared to this point, cooled, covered and refrigerated for up to 1 day. Reheat before continuing.)* Gently stir in parsley; season with salt and pepper to taste. Makes 6 servings.

### BUYING AND STORING VEGETABLES

■ **For maximum flavor, freshness and nutrients, buy vegetables unpackaged and plan to use them within a few days.**

■ **Vegetables start to lose their natural sweetness soon after picking, so buy garden produce from roadside stands or country markets in season.**

■ **Store most vegetables in the refrigerator until you are ready to eat them. Tomatoes should be allowed to ripen at room temperature, and potatoes should be stored in a dark, dry and cool (but not refrigerated) place to prevent sprouting.**

## Apricot-Wild Rice Casserole

*This dish, inspired by wild rice stuffing, goes well with roast chicken, turkey or pork.*

| | | |
|---|---|---|
| 4 cups | water | 1 L |
| 1/2 cup | wild rice, rinsed | 125 mL |
| 2 tsp | vegetable oil | 10 mL |
| 1 cup | chopped onions | 250 mL |
| 1 cup | chopped celery | 250 mL |
| 3/4 cup | parboiled long grain rice | 175 mL |
| 1-1/2 cups | chicken stock | 375 mL |
| 1/2 tsp | each dried sage, savory and thyme | 2 mL |
| 1/3 cup | chopped dried apricots | 75 mL |
| 2 tbsp | currants | 25 mL |
| 1 tsp | grated orange rind | 5 mL |
| 2 tbsp | chopped fresh parsley | 25 mL |
| | Salt and pepper | |

**Per Serving:**

Calories: 150

Fat: 1.6 g

Protein: 4.2 g

Carbohydrate: 30 g

Calcium: 31 mg

Iron: 1.3 mg

Fiber: 2 g

Sodium: 399 mg

Cholesterol: 0 mg

■ In saucepan, bring water to boil; add wild rice. Cover and reduce heat; simmer for 35 to 45 minutes or until tender. Drain.

■ Meanwhile, in heavy saucepan, heat oil over medium-high heat; cook onions and celery until softened, about 3 minutes. Add long grain rice; cook, stirring, for 1 minute.

■ Stir in stock, sage, savory and thyme; bring to boil. Cover and reduce heat; simmer for 10 minutes. Stir in apricots and currants; simmer, covered, for 10 to 15 minutes or until rice is tender and liquid absorbed. Remove from heat.

■ Stir in cooked wild rice, orange rind, parsley, and salt and pepper to taste. *(Recipe can be cooled, covered and refrigerated for up to 2 days. Reheat in 8-cup/2 L covered casserole in 350°F/180°C oven for 30 minutes or until heated through.)* Makes 8 servings.

# Warm Seafood and Chicken Salad

*You can prepare and refrigerate all the ingredients for this salad early in the morning, then stir-fry at the last minute.*

**Per Serving:**

Calories: 211

Fat: 7.8 g

Protein: 18.3 g

Carbohydrate: 17.9 g

Calcium: 87 mg

Iron: 2.1 mg

Fiber: 2.6 g

Sodium: 331 mg

Cholesterol: 43 mg

| | | |
|---|---|---|
| 2 | boneless skinless chicken breasts | 2 |
| 1 lb | mixed seafood (scallops and shrimp) | 500 g |
| 2 tbsp | vegetable oil | 25 mL |
| 1/3 cup | mirin (rice wine for cooking) | 75 mL |
| 3 tbsp | lemon or lime juice | 50 mL |
| 3 tbsp | teriyaki sauce | 50 mL |
| 2 tbsp | granulated sugar | 25 mL |
| 1 tbsp | cornstarch | 15 mL |
| 1 tsp | grated lemon or lime rind | 5 mL |
| 1 tsp | sesame oil | 5 mL |
| | Hot pepper sauce | |
| 3 | oranges, peeled and sliced | 3 |
| 1 | green apple (unpeeled), chopped | 1 |
| 1 | small sweet red or green pepper, slivered | 1 |
| 5 cups | torn mixed salad greens (romaine lettuce, spinach, watercress) | 1.25 L |
| 1/2 cup | toasted sliced almonds* | 125 mL |

■ Slice chicken across the grain into 1/4-inch (5 mm) wide strips. Halve large scallops; peel and devein shrimp.

■ In wok or large skillet, heat oil over high heat; stir-fry chicken for about 4 minutes or until no longer pink inside. Using slotted spoon, remove chicken and keep warm. Add scallops and shrimp to skillet; stir-fry for 3 to 4 minutes or just until scallops are opaque and shrimp are pink. Remove and keep warm.

■ Mix together mirin, lemon juice, teriyaki sauce, sugar, cornstarch, lemon rind, sesame oil, and hot pepper sauce to taste. Add to skillet and bring to boil, stirring constantly; remove from heat.

■ Return reserved chicken and seafood to skillet. Add oranges, apple and red pepper; stir to coat. Mound greens on serving platter; spoon warm mixture on top. Sprinkle with almonds and serve immediately. Makes 8 servings.

*To toast almonds, bake on baking sheet in 350°F (180°C) oven for 10 minutes or until golden.

# Gingery Sweet Potato Bake

*Preserved ginger adds a welcome tang to an old favorite — sweet potatoes.*

**Per Serving:**

Calories: 152

Fat: 0.9 g

Protein: 2.0 g

Carbohydrate: 35.3 g

Calcium: 33 mg

Iron: 0.9 mg

Fiber: 3.2 g

Sodium: 20 mg

Cholesterol: 0 mg

| | | |
|---|---|---|
| 4 | sweet potatoes (about 2 lb/1 kg) | 4 |
| 1 tsp | margarine or butter | 5 mL |
| 1/2 cup | sliced leeks | 125 mL |
| 1 | can (14 oz/398 mL) pineapple chunks (packed in unsweetened juice) | 1 |
| 1/2 tsp | cinnamon | 2 mL |
| 1/4 tsp | nutmeg | 1 mL |
| 1/4 tsp | pepper | 1 mL |
| 4 tsp | finely chopped preserved ginger | 20 mL |

■ Peel sweet potatoes; cut into 1/4-inch (5 mm) thick slices. In skillet, melt margarine or butter over medium heat; cook leeks, covered, for 3 to 5 minutes or until softened. (Alternatively, microwave at High for 2 minutes.)

■ Drain pineapple, reserving juice. Mix together cinnamon, nutmeg and pepper. In 8-cup (2 L) lightly greased casserole, layer half of the sweet potato, pineapple chunks, leeks, spice mixture and ginger. Repeat. Pour reserved pineapple juice over top.

■ Cover and bake in 325°F (160°C) oven for about 1-1/2 hours or until potatoes are tender, basting 2 or 3 times. Uncover for last 15 minutes of baking. Makes 8 servings.

# Vegetable Pasta Salad

**Per Serving:**

Calories: 401

Fat: 6.3 g

Protein: 14.9 g

Carbohydrate: 71.3 g

Calcium: 132 mg

Iron: 2.4 mg

Fiber: 4.1 g

Sodium: 301 mg

Cholesterol: 4 mg

*Vary the flavor of this salad by changing the vegetables. Use asparagus in season, in place of broccoli. Julienned carrots or blanched snow peas can be used instead of zucchini. Any small pasta can be used instead of cartwheels.*

| | | |
|---|---|---|
| 1 cup | broccoli florets | 250 mL |
| 4 cups | cartwheel pasta (3/4 lb/375 g) | 1 L |
| 1 tbsp | vegetable oil | 15 mL |
| 3 | cloves garlic, minced | 3 |
| 1/2 tsp | dried oregano | 2 mL |
| 1/2 cup | taco sauce | 125 mL |
| 1/4 cup | freshly grated Parmesan cheese | 50 mL |
| 1 | baby yellow zucchini, julienned | 1 |
| 1 | small sweet red pepper, seeded and thinly sliced | 1 |
| | Salt and pepper | |

■ In saucepan of boiling water, blanch broccoli for 1 minute; drain and refresh under cold water. Drain again and set aside.

■ In pot of boiling water, cook pasta until tender but firm; drain and transfer to bowl.

■ Meanwhile, in small nonstick skillet or saucepan, heat oil over medium-low heat; cook garlic and oregano for about 3 minutes or until garlic is softened. Toss with pasta.

■ Add taco sauce and Parmesan; toss to mix. Add broccoli, zucchini and red pepper; toss again. Season with salt and pepper to taste. Makes 4 servings.

*Warm Seafood and Chicken Salad*

# Warm Salmon and Asparagus Salad

**Per Serving:**

Calories: 357

Fat: 25 g

Protein: 25.5 g

Carbohydrate: 8.7 g

Calcium: 267 mg

Iron: 2.2 mg

Fiber: 2.3 g

Sodium: 749 mg

Cholesterol: 38 mg

*A light lemony dressing is drizzled over asparagus and salmon for a delightful combination. You can substitute escarole, Bibb or Belgian endive for the iceberg lettuce if desired.*

| | | |
|---|---|---|
| 1 | can (7-1/2 oz/213 g salmon) | 1 |
| 1 | small head iceberg lettuce, shredded | 1 |
| 1 lb | cooked asparagus or broccoli florets | 500 g |
| 1 | carrot, julienned (optional) | 1 |
| 4 | cherry tomatoes (optional) | 4 |

**Dressing:**

| | | |
|---|---|---|
| 2 tbsp | vegetable oil | 25 mL |
| 2 tbsp | apple cider vinegar | 25 mL |
| 2 tbsp | finely chopped onion | 25 mL |
| 1 tbsp | chopped fresh parsley | 15 mL |
| 1 tbsp | lemon juice | 15 mL |
| 1/2 tsp | grated lemon rind | 2 mL |
| 1/2 tsp | granulated sugar | 2 mL |
| 1/4 tsp | salt | 1 mL |
| 1/4 tsp | dried basil | 1 mL |
| | Pepper | |

■ Drain salmon, reserving 2 tbsp (25 mL) liquid. Divide lettuce and salmon among 4 plates. Arrange asparagus on top; garnish with carrot and tomatoes (if using).

**Dressing:** In saucepan, combine reserved salmon liquid, oil, vinegar, onion, parsley, lemon juice and rind, sugar, salt, basil and pepper to taste; bring to boil over medium-high heat, stirring occasionally. Pour over individual salads. Serve immediately. Makes 4 servings.

*Warm Salmon and Asparagus Salad*

## Oriental Vegetable Stir-Fry

**Per Serving:**

Calories: 106

Fat: 5.1 g

Protein: 4.1 g

Carbohydrate: 12.8 g

Calcium: 96 mg

Iron: 2.1 mg

Fiber: 4.7 g

Sodium: 177 mg

Cholesterol: 0 mg

*Ingredients for a stir-fry can be as varied as you wish. Just remember to slice vegetables that require long cooking extra thin and start cooking them first.*

| | | |
|---|---|---|
| 1 tbsp | plum sauce | 15 mL |
| 1 tsp | soy sauce | 5 mL |
| 1/2 tsp | cornstarch | 2 mL |
| | Vegetable or chicken stock | |
| 2 tsp | vegetable oil | 10 mL |
| 2 tsp | sesame oil | 10 mL |
| 2 | cloves garlic, minced | 2 |
| 1 tbsp | finely chopped hot banana pepper | 15 mL |
| 1 tsp | minced gingerroot | 5 mL |
| 1/2 cup | diagonally sliced carrots | 125 mL |
| 1 cup | thinly sliced acorn squash* | 250 mL |
| 1 cup | snow peas | 250 mL |
| 8 | green onions (white and pale green parts), halved crosswise | 8 |
| 1 cup | broccoli florets | 250 mL |
| | Pepper | |

■ In 1 cup (250 mL) measure, blend plum sauce, soy sauce and cornstarch; stir in enough stock to make 2/3 cup (150 mL). Set aside.

■ In nonstick wok or large skillet, heat vegetable and sesame oils over medium-high heat; stir-fry garlic, banana pepper and gingerroot for 30 seconds. Add carrots; stir-fry for 1 minute. Add squash; stir-fry for 1 minute. Add snow peas and onions; stir-fry for 1 minute. Add broccoli; stir-fry for 1 minute.

■ Stir stock mixture and add to pan; cook, stirring, until thickened. Cook, stirring, for 1 minute longer or until vegetables are tender-crisp. Season with pepper to taste. Makes 4 servings.

*Cut squash into pieces approximately same size as carrot slices.

## Risotto-Style Rice

*Arborio, a short grain Italian rice, gives this dish a distinct nutty flavor but you can use any short grain rice in this recipe.*

| | | |
|---|---|---|
| 1 tbsp | margarine or butter | 15 mL |
| 1 tbsp | olive oil | 15 mL |
| 1 | onion, coarsely chopped | 1 |
| 1-1/4 cups | arborio rice | 300 mL |
| 2-1/4 cups | chicken stock | 550 mL |
| 1/4 cup | freshly grated romano or Parmesan cheese | 50 mL |
| | Nutmeg | |
| | Pepper | |

■ In nonstick saucepan, melt margarine or butter with oil over medium-low heat; add onion and stir to coat. Cover and cook for 3 minutes or until softened. Add rice and cook, stirring, for 1 minute to coat. Stir in stock and bring to boil; reduce heat to medium-low, cover and cook for 20 minutes or until rice is tender. Stir in cheese; season with nutmeg and pepper to taste. Makes 4 servings.

**Per Serving:**

Calories: 308

Fat: 8.7 g

Protein: 8.8 g

Carbohydrate: 47 g

Calcium: 100 mg

Iron: 0.8 mg

Fiber: 1.3 g

Sodium: 1261 mg

Cholesterol: 4 mg

---

**VITAMIN C — IT'S EVERYWHERE!**

Citrus fruits (oranges, grapefruit, lemons and limes) are excellent sources of vitamin C. The following foods are high in vitamin C — and they're grown right here in Canada! Values given are for single servings.

| Food | Vitamin C (mg) |
|---|---|
| 1/4 medium cantaloupe | 56 |
| 1/2 cup (125 mL) brussels sprouts, cooked | 51 |
| 1/2 cup (125 mL) broccoli spears, cooked | 51 |
| 1/2 cup (125 mL) apple juice (vitamin C added) | 43 |
| 1/2 cup (125 mL) cauliflower, raw | 38 |
| 1/2 cup (125 mL) strawberries, frozen | 32 |
| 1 medium sweet potato, baked | 28 |

# Refreshing Desserts

**C**ool and creamy Frozen Fruit Yogurt, crispy Lemon Ginger Thins, sinfully light Strawberry Shortcake crowned with sweet summer berries. . .What a perfect way to end a meal. And what a great way to satisfy your sweet tooth without adding lots of calories and fat. Each of the tempting light desserts in this section is loaded with flavor — *and* nutrients! We've included lightened versions of family favorites like Lemony Rice Pudding, as well as appealing new variations on parfaits, crumbles and fruit sherbets.

## Frozen Fruit Yogurt

**Per Serving:**

Calories: 121

Fat: 0.6 g

Protein: 1.8 g

Carbohydrate: 28.9 g

Calcium: 89 mg

Iron: 0.4 mg

Fiber: 2.1 g

Sodium: 14 mg

Cholesterol: 1 mg

*Fresh summer fruits make a delicious colorful frozen yogurt that's low in fat. To make 2 cups (500 mL) stewed rhubarb, cook 4 cups (1 L) chopped rhubarb with 1/2 cup (125 mL) water over medium-high heat for 10 to 15 minutes or until softened.*

| | | |
|---|---|---|
| 2 cups | **unsweetened stewed rhubarb** | 500 mL |
| 2 cups | **strawberries** | 500 mL |
| 1/2 cup | **granulated sugar** | 125 mL |
| 2 tbsp | **orange juice** | 25 mL |
| 1/2 cup | **low-fat yogurt** | 125 mL |

**Strawberry Sauce:**

| | | |
|---|---|---|
| 1/2 cup | **water** | 125 mL |
| 1/2 cup | **raspberry juice concentrate** | 125 mL |
| 2 tbsp | **lemon juice** | 25 mL |
| 1 tbsp | **cornstarch** | 15 mL |
| 1/2 cup | **chopped strawberries** | 125 mL |
| | **Red food coloring (optional)** | |

■ In blender or food processor, purée rhubarb, strawberries, sugar and orange juice; blend in yogurt. Freeze in ice-cream maker following manufacturer's instructions. (Alternatively, pour into 13- × 9-inch/3.5 L cake pan; cover and freeze for about 6 hours or until firm. Break up mixture and process in blender or food processor, in batches if necessary, until smooth and creamy. Place in chilled airtight container and freeze for about 1 hour or until firm.) Let soften for 30 minutes in refrigerator before serving with sauce.

**Strawberry Sauce:** In saucepan, combine water, raspberry concentrate and lemon juice. Whisk in cornstarch; cook over medium-high heat, whisking constantly, until thickened and glossy, 3 to 5 minutes. Transfer to bowl and let cool to room temperature. Stir in chopped strawberries, and food coloring (if using).

■ Spoon sauce over frozen yogurt. Makes 8 servings.

*Frozen Fruit Yogurt*

## Mint-Marinated Fruit

**Per Serving:**

Calories: 205

Fat: 0.6 g

Protein: 1.3 g

Carbohydrate: 53.8 g

Calcium: 28 mg

Iron: 0.6 mg

Fiber: 2.7 g

Sodium: 3 mg

Cholesterol: 0 mg

*This marinated fruit, flavored with mint, honey, lime and orange, is delicious simply served cold. For an unusual accompaniment to grilled meat (or with vanilla ice cream for dessert), thread the fruit onto skewers and heat on the barbecue until glazed.*

| | | |
|---|---|---|
| 2 | **peaches or nectarines** | 2 |
| 2 | **apples** | 2 |
| 2 | **oranges** | 2 |
| 2 | **bananas** | 2 |
| 1 | **small pineapple** | 1 |

**Marinade/Sauce:**

| | | |
|---|---|---|
| 3/4 cup | **liquid honey** | 175 mL |
| 1/2 cup | **lime juice** | 125 mL |
| 1/2 cup | **orange juice** | 125 mL |
| 1/4 cup | **orange liqueur (optional)** | 50 mL |
| 2 tbsp | **chopped fresh mint** | 25 mL |

■ If serving cold, peel peaches, apples, oranges, bananas and pineapple; cut into bite-size pieces. If serving hot, cut unpeeled peaches, apples and oranges into large wedges. Peel bananas and cut into large chunks. Cut pineapple into large cubes, leaving skin on. Place fruit in shallow bowl.

**Marinade/Sauce:** Mix together honey, lime and orange juices, liqueur (if using) and mint; pour over fruit. Marinate for 30 minutes, stirring occasionally.

■ If serving cold, cover and chill for up to 4 hours. To serve hot, thread chunks of fruit alternately on skewers. Pour sauce into small pan and heat on barbecue grill. Grill fruit over medium-hot coals for 5 to 10 minutes or until hot and lightly glazed, turning occasionally and brushing often with sauce. Serve fruit with remaining sauce. Makes 8 servings.

*Mint-Marinated Fruit*

116

# Baked Bananas with Rum and Lemon

**Per Serving:**

Calories: 211

Fat: 1.5 g

Protein: 3.7 g

Carbohydrate: 45.5 g

Calcium: 15 mg

Iron: 0.6 mg

Fiber: 2.1 g

Sodium: 52 mg

Cholesterol: 0 mg

*You can make this rich-tasting dessert in less than 30 minutes.*

| 1/4 cup | dark rum | 50 mL |
|---|---|---|
| 1 tbsp | lemon juice | 15 mL |
| 2 tbsp | packed brown sugar | 25 mL |
| 1 tsp | margarine or butter | 5 mL |
| Pinch | cinnamon | Pinch |
| 4 | bananas | 4 |
| 3 | egg whites | 3 |
| 1/4 cup | granulated sugar | 50 mL |

■ In saucepan over medium heat, combine rum, 2 tsp (10 mL) of the lemon juice, brown sugar, margarine or butter and cinnamon; heat gently until margarine or butter has melted and sugar dissolved.

■ Peel bananas and cut in half lengthwise; arrange in lightly buttered 8-inch (2 L) square baking dish. Pour sauce over; set aside.

■ In bowl, beat egg whites until soft peaks form; sprinkle with remaining lemon juice. Gradually beat in granulated sugar until stiff peaks form. Spoon meringue over bananas, spreading to edges of dish and swirling into mounds. Bake in 350°F (180°C) oven for 10 to 12 minutes or until meringue is golden. Serve warm. Makes 4 servings.

---

**GO BANANAS!**

**Rich in potassium and surprisingly low in calories, bananas are at their best any time of the year. Whether you pack them into lunch boxes or cut them up into fruit salads or custards, bananas are a tasty and satisfying dessert the whole family can enjoy.**

**Buy slightly green bananas and let them ripen at room temperature. Once they are ripe, they should be stored in the refrigerator.**

---

# Poached Pears in Cranberry Juice

*Cranberry juice adds a tart flavor and a light blush to the pears. Diluted apple juice or white grape juice can be used instead without adding color to the pears.*

| 4 | firm ripe pears (about 1-3/4 lb/875 g) | 4 |
|---|---|---|
| 1/4 cup | lemon juice | 50 mL |
| 1/2 cup | cranberry juice | 125 mL |
| 2 tbsp | granulated sugar | 25 mL |
| 2 tbsp | orange juice | 25 mL |
| 1 tsp | finely grated orange rind | 5 mL |

**Per Serving:**

Calories: 141

Fat: 0.6 g

Protein: 0.7 g

Carbohydrate: 36.5 g

Calcium: 20 mg

Iron: 0.5 mg

Fiber: 4.9 g

Sodium: 2 mg

Cholesterol: 0 mg

■ Halve, peel and core pears; brush all over with lemon juice. In nonaluminum skillet large enough to hold pears in single layer, bring cranberry juice, sugar, orange juice and rind to simmer; add pears and return to simmer.

■ Cover and cook for 20 to 25 minutes or until pears are tender, turning pears over halfway through cooking time. Transfer to serving bowl and let cool, turning pears over occasionally. Serve at room temperature or chilled. Makes 4 servings.

## Microwave method:

■ Halve, peel and core pears; brush all over with lemon juice. In 8-cup (2 L) microwaveable casserole, arrange pear halves in spoke-fashion with thicker ends toward outside.

■ Using only 1/4 cup (50 mL) cranberry juice, combine with sugar, orange juice and rind; pour over pears. Cover and microwave at High for 4 minutes; baste, turn pears over and rotate dish once. Microwave, covered, at High for 4 to 6 minutes or until tender. Uncover and let cool, turning pears over occasionally. Makes 4 servings.

## Angel Food Cake

*This light-as-a-cloud cake is delicious on its own — or serve it with Raspberry Fruit Sauce (recipe follows).*

| | | |
|---|---|---|
| 6 | egg whites | 6 |
| 1/2 tsp | cream of tartar | 2 mL |
| Pinch | salt | Pinch |
| 1 cup | granulated sugar | 250 mL |
| 3/4 cup | sifted cake-and-pastry flour | 175 mL |

■ In large bowl, beat egg whites until foamy. Add cream of tartar and salt; beat until soft peaks form. Gradually beat in 1/2 cup (125 mL) of the sugar until stiff peaks form.

■ Sift together flour and remaining sugar; fold into egg whites, about one-third at a time, incorporating each completely. Pour into ungreased 9- × 5-inch (2 L) loaf pan; bake in 325°F (160°C) oven for 40 to 45 minutes or until cake is golden and top springs back when lightly touched.

■ Turn pan upside down and, supporting pan at corners, let cake hang until completely cooled. Run knife around edges of pan to loosen cake and remove from pan. If desired, serve with Raspberry Fruit Sauce. Makes 8 servings.

**Per Serving (Cake Only):**

Calories: 147

Fat: 0.1 g

Protein: 3.3 g

Carbohydrate: 33.7 g

Calcium: 5 mg

Iron: 0.4 mg

Fiber: 0.3 g

Sodium: 38 mg

Cholesterol: 0 mg

### Raspberry Fruit Sauce:

| | | |
|---|---|---|
| 2 cups | raspberry juice | 500 mL |
| 1 tbsp | cornstarch | 15 mL |
| 1 | large pear, peeled and sliced | 1 |
| 1 | orange, sectioned | 1 |
| 1 | small banana, sliced | 1 |

■ In saucepan, blend raspberry juice with cornstarch; bring to simmer, stirring constantly. Cook over medium heat, stirring, until thickened and clear. Remove from heat; gently stir in pear, orange and banana. Makes 4 cups (1 L), enough for 8 servings.

**Per Serving:**

Calories: 68

Fat: 0.2 g

Protein: 0.5 g

Carbohydrate: 17.3 g

Calcium: 12 mg

Iron: 0.2 mg

Fiber: 1.3 g

Sodium: 0 mg

Cholesterol: 0 mg

## Yogurt and Fresh Fruit Parfait

*Layer fresh berries and sliced fruit — such as peaches, apricots, kiwifruit, pineapple and mango — between creamy yogurt custard for a light, low-fat dessert.*

| | | |
|---|---|---|
| 1/3 cup | granulated sugar | 75 mL |
| 2 tbsp | cornstarch | 25 mL |
| 1-1/2 tsp | unflavored gelatin | 7 mL |
| 2 tsp | grated lemon rind | 10 mL |
| 1 cup | 2% milk | 250 mL |
| 1 cup | low-fat yogurt | 250 mL |
| 1 tsp | vanilla | 5 mL |
| 2 cups | fresh berries or sliced fruit | 500 mL |

■ In small saucepan, stir together sugar, cornstarch, gelatin and lemon rind; stir in milk. Cook, stirring, over medium heat until thickened and smooth; cook, stirring, for 2 minutes longer. Remove from heat. Gradually stir in yogurt; add vanilla. Refrigerate, stirring occasionally, for about 1 hour or until consistency of thick custard and thoroughly cooled. With electric mixer, beat for 1 minute. Spoon into 4 parfait glasses alternately with fruit, starting and ending with custard. Makes 4 servings.

**Per Serving:**

Calories: 194

Fat: 2.4 g

Protein: 6.6 g

Carbohydrate: 37.6 g

Calcium: 197 mg

Iron: 0.4 mg

Fiber: 1.6 g

Sodium: 76 mg

Cholesterol: 8 mg

### RHUBARB

**Select firm cherry red or pink stalks. Small or medium stalks are more tender than large ones. Use rhubarb within a few days of picking or purchase. Cut off and discard leaves (which are poisonous) and whitish stem ends. Refrigerate stalks in moisture-proof container or plastic bag. Do not peel the stalks; just wash before cutting into pieces. The skin provides color and helps to hold the pieces of rhubarb in shape during cooking.**

## Rhubarb-Strawberry Mould with Yogurt Sauce

**Per Serving:**

Calories: 175

Fat: 1.1 g

Protein: 5.5 g

Carbohydrate: 37.4 g

Calcium: 173 mg

Iron: 0.6 mg

Fiber: 1.8 g

Sodium: 48 mg

Cholesterol: 4 mg

*Believe it or not, one cup (250 mL) of stewed rhubarb contains more calcium than the same measure of whole milk.*

| | | |
|---|---|---|
| 2 | **envelopes unflavored gelatin** | 2 |
| 1/2 cup | **orange juice** | 125 mL |
| 4 cups | **chopped rhubarb (about 1 lb/500 g)** | 1 L |
| 3/4 cup | **granulated sugar** | 175 mL |
| 1 | **pkg (300 g) frozen sliced strawberries** | 1 |

**Yogurt Sauce:**

| | | |
|---|---|---|
| 2 cups | **low-fat yogurt** | 500 mL |
| 1/4 cup | **granulated sugar** | 50 mL |
| 1 tsp | **cinnamon** | 5 mL |

■ Sprinkle gelatin over orange juice; let stand for 5 minutes to soften.

■ Meanwhile, in heavy nonaluminum saucepan, combine rhubarb with sugar; cover and cook over medium heat, stirring occasionally, for 8 to 10 minutes or until tender. Remove from heat; stir in gelatin, then strawberries.

■ Pour into 6-cup (1.5 L) stainless steel, glass or plastic mould. Cover and refrigerate for at least 4 hours or up to 2 days. Dip bowl in hot water for a few seconds to loosen mould. Invert onto serving plate.

**Yogurt Sauce:** Combine yogurt, sugar and cinnamon. Pass separately to serve with mould. Makes 8 servings.

*Rhubarb-Strawberry Mould with Yogurt Sauce*

119

## Tropical Fruit Salad

**Per Serving:**

Calories: 105

Fat: 0.6 g

Protein: 0.9 g

Carbohydrate: 26.7 g

Calcium: 18 mg

Iron: 0.5 mg

Fiber: 2.4 g

Sodium: 3 mg

Cholesterol: 0 mg

*You can make a fruit salad with a summery touch any time of the year by substituting canned apricots for the mango, frozen black cherries for the grapes and unsweetened frozen raspberries for the strawberries. For our photograph, we garnished the salad with star fruit.*

| | | |
|---|---|---|
| 1/4 cup | lime juice | 50 mL |
| 1 | strip (1/2-in/1 cm wide) lime rind (green part only) | 1 |
| 1/3 cup | water | 75 mL |
| 1/4 cup | granulated sugar | 50 mL |
| 3 cups | fresh pineapple chunks | 750 mL |
| 1 cup | black or red grapes | 250 mL |
| 1 | large mango, peeled and cubed | 1 |
| 2 | small kiwifruit | 2 |
| 1 cup | strawberries | 250 mL |

■ In small saucepan, combine lime juice and rind, water and sugar; bring to boil. (Alternatively, combine in microwaveable measure; microwave at High for 1 minute or until sugar is dissolved.) Discard rind; let cool.

■ In large glass bowl, combine pineapple, grapes and mango; pour in syrup and stir to mix. Cover and refrigerate until chilled. Just before serving, peel and slice kiwifruit; add to bowl. Hull strawberries; add to bowl and mix gently. Makes 8 servings.

*Tropical Fruit Salad*

## Lemony Rice Pudding

**Per Serving:**

Calories: 296

Fat: 4.8 g

Protein: 10.1 g

Carbohydrate: 53.6 g

Calcium: 313 mg

Iron: 0.6 mg

Fiber: 1 g

Sodium: 401 mg

Cholesterol: 18 mg

*High on the list of favorite comfort foods, this old-fashioned dessert is a delicious way to get your daily milk quota. Be sure to use short grain rice — it gives the pudding a smooth, creamy texture.*

| 1/2 cup | short grain rice | 125 mL |
|---------|------------------|--------|
| 4 cups | 2% milk | 1 L |
| 1/4 cup | granulated sugar | 50 mL |
| 1/4 cup | skim milk powder (optional) | 50 mL |
| 1/3 cup | raisins | 75 mL |
| 1 tbsp | finely grated lemon rind | 15 mL |
| Pinch | nutmeg | Pinch |
| 1 tsp | vanilla | 5 mL |

■ In deep saucepan, combine rice, milk, sugar, skim milk powder (if using), raisins, lemon rind and nutmeg. Cover and bring just to boil; stir and reduce heat to medium-low. Simmer, covered and stirring occasionally, for 30 minutes; uncover and simmer, stirring occasionally, for 15 minutes or until rice is tender and mixture has thickened. Stir in vanilla. Makes 4 servings.

---

**BERRIED TREASURE**

**Fresh berries are a perfect light dessert. They're sweet and juicy, easy to prepare, high in fiber and vitamin C — and, best of all, they're fat-free! Serve them alone or with other fruits in a refreshing fruit salad. Or top them with fresh or frozen low-fat yogurt.**

**Berries are at their prime nutritionally when they're fully ripe with a deep even color. Enjoy berries as soon as possible after they've been picked or purchased. If they have to be stored, refrigerate without washing them.**

---

## Light Strawberry Shortcake

*Thickened yogurt is a delicious low-fat alternative to whipped cream. Team it with angel food cake (recipe, p.118) and fresh berries, and you've got a quick low-cal strawberry shortcake.*

**Per Serving:**

Calories: 130

Fat: 1.1 g

Protein: 5.2 g

Carbohydrate: 25.4 g

Calcium: 118 mg

Iron: 0.4 mg

Fiber: 0.7 g

Sodium: 114 mg

Cholesterol: 4 mg

| 3 cups | low-fat yogurt | 750 mL |
|--------|----------------|--------|
| 3 tbsp | granulated sugar | 50 mL |
| 1 tsp | grated lemon rind | 5 mL |
| 1/2 tsp | vanilla | 2 mL |
| 1 | angel food cake | 1 |
| 2-1/2 cups | sliced fresh strawberries | 625 mL |
| 1 tbsp | icing sugar | 15 mL |

■ In cheesecloth-lined sieve set over bowl, cover yogurt and let drain in refrigerator for at least 12 hours or overnight. Discard liquid. In bowl, blend drained yogurt with granulated sugar, lemon rind and vanilla.

■ Cut cake horizontally into 3 layers. Spread half of the yogurt mixture over first layer. Arrange 1 cup (250 mL) of the berries over yogurt mixture. Cover with second layer, remaining yogurt mixture and 1 cup (250 mL) of the berries. Top with third layer.

■ Dust top with icing sugar; garnish with remaining berries. Makes 12 servings.

## Gingery Crumb Crust

**Per Serving (Crust Only):**

Calories: 93

Fat: 5.4 g

Protein: 0.9 g

Carbohydrate: 10.4 g

Calcium: 4 mg

Iron: 0.5 mg

Fiber: 0.4 g

Sodium: 86 mg

Cholesterol: 0 mg

*A hint of ginger makes this pie crust extra tasty. Add a favorite creamy filling — or fill with Yogurt-Orange Whip (recipe, this page) and garnish with berries.*

| 1 cup | digestive biscuit crumbs | 250 mL |
|---|---|---|
| 1 tbsp | packed brown sugar | 15 mL |
| 1/2 tsp | ground ginger | 2 mL |
| 2 tbsp | margarine or butter, melted | 25 mL |

■ In bowl, mix together biscuit crumbs, sugar and ginger; drizzle with margarine or butter and toss to mix well. Press into 9-inch (23 cm) pie plate. Bake in 350°F (180°C) oven for 10 minutes or until crisp and browned. Makes one pie shell, enough for 8 servings.

## Orange Cream Topping

**Per 1/4-Cup (50 mL) Serving:**

Calories: 60

Fat: 1.1 g

Protein: 7.7 g

Carbohydrate: 4.3 g

Calcium: 39 mg

Iron: 0.1 mg

Fiber: 0 g

Sodium: 229 mg

Cholesterol: 5 mg

*Well-puréed cottage cheese makes a pleasant alternative to whipped cream and has about half the calories. Serve as a topping or a dip with fresh fruit.*

| 1 cup | 2% cottage cheese | 250 mL |
|---|---|---|
| 2 tsp | granulated sugar | 10 mL |
| 1/2 tsp | grated orange rind | 2 mL |
| 1/2 tsp | vanilla | 2 mL |
| Pinch | cinnamon | Pinch |

■ In blender or food processor, blend cottage cheese, sugar, orange rind and vanilla for 2 to 3 minutes or until smooth and creamy.
■ Serve immediately or cover and refrigerate for up to 2 days. Before serving, sprinkle lightly with cinnamon. Makes 1 cup (250 mL).

## Yogurt-Orange Whip with Strawberry Sauce

*Serve this smooth, refreshing dessert on its own or pour yogurt mixture into a Gingery Crumb Crust (recipe, this page) and top with strawberry sauce.*

**Per Serving:**

Calories: 107

Fat: 1.3 g

Protein: 5.5 g

Carbohydrate: 18.7 g

Calcium: 153 mg

Iron: 0.1 mg

Fiber: 0.1 g

Sodium: 59 mg

Cholesterol: 5 mg

| 2 tsp | grated orange rind | 10 mL |
|---|---|---|
| 1 cup | orange juice | 250 mL |
| 1/3 cup | granulated sugar | 75 mL |
| 1 | envelope unflavored gelatin | 1 |
| 2 cups | low-fat yogurt | 500 mL |
| 1 | pkg (300 g) unsweetened frozen strawberries, thawed | 1 |

■ In saucepan, combine orange rind and juice, 1/4 cup (50 mL) of the sugar and gelatin; heat gently until gelatin has dissolved. Transfer to bowl; chill until almost set.
■ Beat gelatin mixture until fluffy; stir in yogurt. Pour into 6 sherbet glasses and chill until firm.
■ In food processor or blender, purée strawberries; stir in remaining sugar. Just before serving, spoon sauce over yogurt mixture. Makes 6 servings.

### POUR IT ON!

There's nothing like the taste of luscious, juicy, just-picked fruits and berries. But while fresh is still best, you can transform the season's sweetness into a variety of fruit sauces — and transform simple desserts into sensational ones. Liven up frozen yogurt and ice cream, angel and pound cakes, and dessert soufflés with the light, easy-to-make raspberry and strawberry sauces in this section.

### DIP IT IN!

Nothing could be simpler or more appealing for dessert than an attractively arranged serving of fruit. Choose one or several fresh fruits in season — strawberries, melon balls, blackberries, pineapple wedges, cherries — and add a cool and creamy dip (see recipe for Orange Cream Topping, this page).

## Date-Stuffed Baked Apples

**Per Serving:**

Calories: 163

Fat: 3 g

Protein: 1.5 g

Carbohydrate: 36.7 g

Calcium: 26 mg

Iron: 0.8 mg

Fiber: 4.1 g

Sodium: 3 mg

Cholesterol: 0 mg

*For a taste variation, use dried figs instead of dates; both are rich in fiber, but figs have slightly more. Cooking time may vary depending on size or variety of apples.*

| 4 | apples | 4 |
|---|---|---|
| 1/2 cup | chopped dates | 125 mL |
| 2 tbsp | finely chopped pecans or walnuts | 25 mL |
| 1 tsp | cinnamon | 5 mL |
| 1/4 cup | orange or apple juice | 50 mL |

■ Core apples; peel one-quarter of way down, then at even intervals vertically score the peel down to base.

■ Mix together dates, pecans and cinnamon; stuff into cored apples, heaping on top if necessary. Arrange in shallow 8-inch (2 L) square or round baking dish. Pour orange juice evenly over date mixture.

■ Pour about 1/2 inch (1 cm) water into pan; loosely cover apples with foil. Bake in 350°F (180°C) oven for about 45 minutes or until apples are tender, basting with pan juices several times during baking. Serve warm or chilled. Makes 4 servings.

*Date-Stuffed Baked Apples*

---

**MENU SUGGESTION**

COD CAKES
*Page 72*

FRESH TOMATO SALSA
*Page 101*

GREEN BEANS

DATE-STUFFED BAKED APPLES
*This Page*

---

# Blueberry Custard Parfaits

**Per Serving:**

Calories: 176

Fat: 5.1 g

Protein: 5 g

Carbohydrate: 28.6 g

Calcium: 123 mg

Iron: 0.3 mg

Fiber: 1.4 g

Sodium: 87 mg

Cholesterol: 61 mg

*Use any fresh berries in season in this dessert. Layer custard with sliced strawberries, halved black cherries, or whole raspberries (red or golden) or blackberries.*

| 1/4 cup | granulated sugar | 50 mL |
|---|---|---|
| 2 tbsp | cornstarch | 25 mL |
| 1-1/2 cups | 2% milk | 375 mL |
| 1 | egg | 1 |
| 2 tsp | lemon juice | 10 mL |
| 2 tsp | grated lemon rind | 10 mL |
| 1/2 tsp | vanilla | 2 mL |
| 2 tsp | margarine or butter | 10 mL |
| 1-1/2 cups | fresh blueberries | 375 mL |

■ In saucepan, combine sugar and cornstarch; blend in milk until smooth. Cook, stirring, over medium-high heat until beginning to thicken. Reduce heat to medium and cook, stirring often, for 2 minutes longer.

■ In small dish, whisk egg with lemon juice; stir in about one-third of the hot mixture. Return to pan along with lemon rind and vanilla. Cook, stirring, for 2 minutes or until thickened. Remove from heat; stir in margarine or butter. Let cool for 5 minutes, stirring often.

■ Spoon half of the custard evenly into 4 parfait glasses. Top each evenly with blueberries, reserving a few for garnish. Cover with remaining custard. Cover loosely with plastic wrap; refrigerate until chilled. Garnish with remaining berries just before serving. Makes 4 servings.

# Cranberry Crumble Dessert

*Cranberries add a tangy taste to this fast and easy dessert. Vary the flavor of the crumble by using 2/3 cup (150 mL) Baked Granola (recipe, p.11) in place of the rolled oats and walnuts in the base of this dessert.*

| 3 cups | cranberries, fresh or frozen | 750 mL |
|---|---|---|
| 3/4 cup | granulated sugar | 175 mL |
| 2 tsp | grated orange rind | 10 mL |
| 1/4 cup | orange juice | 50 mL |
| **Base:** | | |
| 1-1/4 cups | graham cracker crumbs | 300 mL |
| 1/2 cup | rolled oats | 125 mL |
| 2 tbsp | granulated sugar | 25 mL |
| 2 tbsp | finely chopped walnuts | 25 mL |
| 1 tsp | cinnamon | 5 mL |
| 1/4 cup | margarine or butter, melted | 50 mL |

**Per Serving:**

Calories: 252

Fat: 8.8 g

Protein: 2.7 g

Carbohydrate: 43.3 g

Calcium: 21 mg

Iron: 1 mg

Fiber: 2.6 g

Sodium: 178 mg

Cholesterol: 0 mg

■ In heavy saucepan, combine cranberries, sugar, orange rind and juice; bring to boil, stirring. Reduce heat to medium-low; boil gently for 15 minutes or until berries pop and mixture thickens slightly. Let cool for 5 minutes.

**Base:** Meanwhile, in bowl, mix crumbs, rolled oats, sugar, walnuts and cinnamon; stir in melted margarine or butter. Pat two-thirds of the mixture into 8-inch (2 L) square baking dish. Bake in 375°F (190°C) oven for 6 minutes.

■ Spread cranberry filling over base; sprinkle with remaining crumb mixture. Bake for 6 minutes longer. Serve warm or cold. Makes 8 servings.

## Light Peach and Berry Crisp

**Per Serving:**

Calories: 155

Fat: 4.5 g

Protein: 2.3 g

Carbohydrate: 28.2 g

Calcium: 26 mg

Iron: 1.1 mg

Fiber: 3 g

Sodium: 47 mg

Cholesterol: 0 mg

*Serve this light version of an old family favorite with low-fat yogurt, if you wish.*

| | | |
|---|---|---|
| 3 cups | sliced peeled peaches | 750 mL |
| 1 cup | raspberries or blueberries | 250 mL |
| 2 tbsp | all-purpose flour | 25 mL |
| 1 tbsp | granulated sugar | 15 mL |
| 1/3 cup | rolled oats | 75 mL |
| 1/4 cup | packed brown sugar | 50 mL |
| 2 tbsp | oat bran | 25 mL |
| 1 tsp | cinnamon | 5 mL |
| 2 tbsp | margarine or butter | 25 mL |

■ In 8-inch (2 L) square baking dish, combine peaches and raspberries. Combine 1 tbsp (15 mL) of the flour and granulated sugar; stir into fruit. Combine rolled oats, brown sugar, oat bran, remaining flour and cinnamon; cut in margarine or butter until crumbly. Sprinkle over fruit. Bake in 375°F (190°C) oven for 30 to 35 minutes or until peaches are tender and topping is browned and crisp. Makes 6 servings.

### PEACH FACTS

■ **Choose firm peaches with no blemishes or bruises. Select them for a good "ground" color (yellow) rather than for the amount of "blush" (red).**

■ **To peel, plunge peaches into boiling water for 30 to 60 seconds; slip off skins and sprinkle with fresh lemon juice to prevent discoloration.**

*Light Peach and Berry Crisp*

## Oatmeal Raisin Cookies

**Per Cookie:**

Calories: 81

Fat: 3 g

Protein: 1.4 g

Carbohydrate: 13.2 g

Calcium: 12 mg

Iron: 0.5 mg

Fiber: 0.9 g

Sodium: 72 mg

Cholesterol: 6 mg

*These great lunch box cookies are a family favorite. Make an extra batch to have on hand for nutritious snacks.*

| | | |
|---|---|---|
| 1/2 cup | margarine or butter, softened | 125 mL |
| 1/2 cup | granulated sugar | 125 mL |
| 1/2 cup | packed brown sugar | 125 mL |
| 1 | egg | 1 |
| 1 cup | whole wheat flour | 250 mL |
| 1 cup | rolled oats | 250 mL |
| 1/4 cup | wheat germ | 50 mL |
| 1 tsp | baking powder | 5 mL |
| 1 tsp | baking soda | 5 mL |
| 1 cup | raisins | 250 mL |

■ In bowl, cream margarine or butter with granulated and brown sugars; beat in egg. Combine flour, oats, wheat germ, baking powder and baking soda; add to creamed mixture and mix well. Stir in raisins.

■ Drop by tablespoonfuls (15 mL) onto lightly greased baking sheets; flatten slightly with floured fork. Bake in 350°F (180°C) oven for about 12 minutes or until light golden. Makes 3 dozen.

*(bottom left)*
*Oatmeal Raisin*
*Cookies*

## Lemon Ginger Thins

**Per Cookie:**

Calories: 64

Fat: 2.6 g

Protein: 0.8 g

Carbohydrate: 9.5 g

Calcium: 5 mg

Iron: 0.4 mg

Fiber: 0.2 g

Sodium: 2 mg

Cholesterol: 17 mg

*Make a batch of these light lemony cookies on the weekend for the family's weekday lunches.*

| 1 cup | all-purpose flour | 250 mL |
|---|---|---|
| 1 tsp | ginger | 5 mL |
| 1/4 tsp | each nutmeg, cinnamon and cloves | 1 mL |
| 1/4 cup | margarine or butter | 50 mL |
| 1/4 cup | packed brown sugar | 50 mL |
| 1/4 cup | granulated sugar | 50 mL |
| 1 | egg yolk | 1 |
| 1 tsp | grated lemon rind | 5 mL |
| 1 tsp | lemon extract | 5 mL |

■ Sift together flour, ginger, nutmeg, cinnamon and cloves. In separate bowl, cream margarine or butter; add brown and granulated sugars and egg yolk and beat well. Beat in lemon rind and extract. Stir in flour mixture until well blended; gather dough into ball. Wrap in plastic wrap or foil; refrigerate until well chilled, about 1 hour.

■ Divide dough into 4 pieces. On lightly floured surface or between 2 sheets of waxed paper, roll out each piece to 1/8-inch (3 mm) thickness. Using 3-inch (8 cm) round cookie cutter, cut out cookies. Bake on ungreased baking sheets in 350°F (180°C) oven for 6 to 8 minutes or until golden. Let cool on racks, then store in airtight container. Makes 20 cookies.

### FREEZING COOKIES

**To make sure you always have nutritious cookies on hand for desserts, lunch boxes or snacks, bake an extra batch of cookies and freeze them. To freeze baked cookies, place cookies in a single layer in the freezer for about 1 hour or until frozen. Put frozen cookies into freezer containers or bags and keep in freezer for up to 12 months. Pack cookies, frozen, in lunch boxes.**

## Orange Meringue Cookies

*One or two of these cookies will satisfy your craving for something sweet without adding a lot of calories or fat.*

| 1/4 cup | sliced almonds | 50 mL |
|---|---|---|
| 1/2 cup | granulated sugar | 125 mL |
| 1 tbsp | cornstarch | 15 mL |
| 3 | egg whites | 3 |
| 1/4 tsp | cream of tartar | 1 mL |
| 1 tbsp | grated orange rind | 15 mL |

**Per Cookie:**

Calories: 21

Fat: 0.5 g

Protein: 0.5 g

Carbohydrate: 3.8 g

Calcium: 3 mg

Iron: 0 mg

Fiber: 0.1 g

Sodium: 5 mg

Cholesterol: 0 mg

■ Spread almonds on baking sheet; toast in 325°F (160°C) oven for 5 minutes or until golden. Let cool.

■ Mix sugar with cornstarch. In large bowl, beat egg whites until foamy; add cream of tartar and beat until soft peaks form. Beat in sugar mixture, a spoonful at a time until stiff, glossy peaks form. Fold in almonds and orange rind.

■ Drop by tablespoonfuls (15 mL) onto foil-lined baking sheet. Bake in 200°F (100°C) oven for 2 hours; cookies will still be moist. Turn off oven and let meringues dry in oven overnight. (Cookies can be stored in airtight container for up to 1 week. Do not freeze.) Makes 30 cookies.

# Watermelon Sherbet

**Per Serving:**

Calories: 91

Fat: 0.5 g

Protein: 1.9 g

Carbohydrate: 21.2 g

Calcium: 11 mg

Iron: 0.2 mg

Fiber: 0.4 g

Sodium: 19 mg

Cholesterol: 0 mg

*To capture the fresh flavor and smooth texture of homemade sherbet, make and serve within 2 days. Round out this refreshing dessert with some simple ice cream wafers — or try Lemon Ginger Thins or Orange Meringue Cookies (recipes, p.127).*

| 4 cups | cubed watermelon | 1 L |
|--------|------------------|-----|
| 1/4 cup | frozen raspberry juice concentrate | 50 mL |
| 1/4 cup | lemon juice | 50 mL |
| 2 | egg whites | 2 |
| Pinch | salt | Pinch |
| 1/4 cup | granulated sugar | 50 mL |

■ In food processor or blender, purée watermelon to make about 3 cups (750 mL). Strain into bowl; stir in raspberry concentrate and lemon juice.

■ In bowl, beat egg whites with salt until foamy; gradually beat in sugar until stiff peaks form. Gently whisk in watermelon mixture.

■ Pour into canister of ice-cream maker and freeze according to manufacturer's instructions. (Alternatively, pour into 8-inch/2 L square baking pan. Cover and freeze for about 6 hours or until firm; mixture will separate into 2 layers during freezing. Break up mixture and process, in batches if necessary, in food processor fitted with metal blade until smooth and creamy. Place in chilled airtight container and freeze for about 1 hour or until firm.) Makes 6 servings.

### SERVING SHERBET

**Sherbets are easier to scoop and taste better when not solidly frozen. About two hours before serving, break frozen sherbet into chunks; beat with electric mixer (or purée in food processor or blender) and freeze. The result is sherbet with a smooth, soft texture that's easy to spoon into parfait glasses or pretty dessert bowls.**

*Watermelon
Sherbet*

# Grape Sorbet with Melon and Ginger

*Serve this pretty dessert in tall glasses or scalloped melon shells.*

**Per Serving:**

Calories: 123

Fat: 0.2 g

Protein: 0.8 g

Carbohydrate: 31.8 g

Calcium: 12 mg

Iron: 0.2 mg

Fiber: 1.2 g

Sodium: 17 mg

Cholesterol: 0 mg

| 1 | large honeydew melon | 1 |
|---|----------------------|---|
| 1 cup | unsweetened white grape juice | 250 mL |
| 1/2 cup | granulated sugar | 125 mL |
| 1 tsp | grated lemon rind | 5 mL |
| 2 tbsp | lemon juice | 25 mL |
| 1 | piece (1 inch/2.5 cm) gingerroot, thinly sliced | 1 |
| | Small bunches of green grapes | |
| | Sprigs of fern | |

■ Cut melon in half and remove seeds. Scoop out pulp and reserve 2 cups (500 mL). Refrigerate remainder for another use.

■ In nonaluminum saucepan, combine grape juice, sugar, lemon rind, lemon juice and gingerroot. Bring to boil; reduce heat and simmer for 5 minutes. With slotted spoon, remove and discard gingerroot.

■ In food processor or blender, combine juice mixture with reserved melon; process until smooth. Pour into shallow dish; freeze until firm. Break into chunks and process again until smooth and thick. Pack into covered container and freeze until firm, at least 4 hours. (Alternatively, freeze in ice-cream maker according to manufacturer's instructions.)

■ Scoop sorbet into sherbet glasses; garnish with grapes and fern. Makes 8 servings.

# Good-for-you Snacks

**H**ere's a tempting array of appealing light bites — just right for when the urge to snack strikes. We've included low-calorie, low-fat Whole Wheat Pretzels and Crunchy Seed Cookies, as well as satisfying Apricot Snacking Cake and Crunchy Banana Bread. And our low-fat, low-salt Quick Vegetable Pizza is perfect for weekend snacking or busy weekday dinners. Just add a green salad or bowls of steaming soup to make it a meal.

## Power Pack Snack

**Per 1/4-Cup
(50 mL)
Serving:**

Calories: 62

Fat: 1.4 g

Protein: 1.6 g

Carbohydrate: 12.1 g

Calcium: 10 mg

Iron: 1 mg

Fiber: 1.4 g

Sodium: 33 mg

Cholesterol: 0 mg

*Munching on this breakfast snack will provide a much better start to the day than an empty stomach. It's great after school, too.*

| | | |
|---|---|---|
| 2 cups | small-size shredded wheat cereal | 500 mL |
| 2 cups | bran flakes cereal | 500 mL |
| 1 cup | raisins | 250 mL |
| 1/2 cup | chopped dried apricots | 125 mL |
| 1/2 cup | sunflower seeds or nuts | 125 mL |
| 1/2 cup | banana chips (optional) | 125 mL |

■ In large bowl, combine shredded wheat, bran flakes, raisins, apricots, sunflower seeds, and banana chips (if using); mix well. Transfer to large jar or airtight container. Serve as snack or breakfast cereal. Makes about 7 cups (1.75 L).

---

**SKINNY SNACKS**

Each of these great-tasting and satisfying snacks weighs in at about 100 calories or less:

■ 2 cups (500 mL) unbuttered popcorn

■ a hard-cooked egg

■ a banana, orange or pear

■ 1/2 cantaloupe

■ 3/4 cup (200 mL) juice-packed pineapple chunks

■ 1/2 cup (125 mL) low-fat frozen yogurt

■ 1/2 unbuttered English muffin with jam

■ 2 melba toast with 1/2 oz (15 g) cheese

■ 1 slice raisin bread, lightly spread with margarine or butter

■ a handful of grapes

■ 2 wheat thins with 2 tsp (10 mL) peanut butter

■ 4 crackers and 1 cup (250 mL) tomato or vegetable juice

*Power Pack
Snack*

## Quick Vegetable Pizza

**Per Serving:**

Calories: 402

Fat: 19.2 g

Protein: 21.3 g

Carbohydrate: 37.4 g

Calcium: 524 mg

Iron: 3.6 mg

Fiber: 4.5 g

Sodium: 682 mg

Cholesterol: 36 mg

*Pizza — a favorite fast food — is well balanced since it contains something from all four food groups. Commercial ones, however, can be high in fat and salt so here's a tasty alternative. It starts with a long flatbread, 2 split 8-inch (20 cm) pita breads or 4 tortillas as a base. If Lappi cheese is unavailable, use Fontina, Edam or Gouda.*

| | | |
|---|---|---|
| 1 tbsp | margarine or butter | 15 mL |
| 1 tbsp | vegetable oil | 15 mL |
| 1 cup | chopped onion | 250 mL |
| 1/2 cup | chopped fresh parsley | 125 mL |
| 1 | clove garlic, minced | 1 |
| Pinch | dried thyme | Pinch |
| 4 cups | torn spinach | 1 L |
| 1 | long flatbread | 1 |
| 1 cup | each thinly sliced cooked potatoes and zucchini | 250 mL |
| 1 cup | chopped seeded drained canned tomatoes | 250 mL |
| | Pepper | |
| 2 cups | shredded Lappi cheese | 500 mL |
| 2 tbsp | freshly grated Parmesan cheese | 25 mL |

■ In heavy saucepan, melt margarine or butter with oil over medium heat; cook onion, parsley, garlic and thyme, stirring, for 1 minute. Reduce heat to medium-low; cover and cook for 5 minutes or until onion is softened. Increase heat to medium-high; add spinach, about a cup at a time, and cook, stirring constantly, until wilted and liquid has evaporated.

■ On baking sheet, spread spinach mixture evenly over flatbread; arrange potatoes, zucchini and tomatoes on top. Season with pepper to taste. Sprinkle with Lappi cheese, then Parmesan; bake in 400°F (200°C) oven for 15 minutes or until cheese is melted. Makes 4 servings.

## Muffins-in-a-Square

*Spreading the batter in a pan is faster and simpler than filling muffin cups. And the squares wrap well for toting to school or work.*

| | | |
|---|---|---|
| 1/2 cup | all-purpose flour | 125 mL |
| 1/2 cup | cornmeal | 125 mL |
| 1/2 cup | quick-cooking rolled oats | 125 mL |
| 1/2 cup | packed brown sugar | 125 mL |
| 1/4 cup | whole wheat flour | 50 mL |
| 1/4 cup | oat bran | 50 mL |
| 1/4 cup | 100% bran cereal | 50 mL |
| 2 tsp | baking powder | 10 mL |
| 1 tsp | baking soda | 5 mL |
| 1 tsp | cinnamon | 5 mL |
| 1/2 tsp | salt | 2 mL |
| 1 | egg | 1 |
| 1 | apple, unpeeled and grated | 1 |
| 3/4 cup | 2% milk | 175 mL |
| 2 tbsp | vegetable oil | 25 mL |
| 2 tbsp | wheat germ | 25 mL |

**Per Square:**

Calories: 111

Fat: 2.8 g

Protein: 2.9 g

Carbohydrate: 19.3 g

Calcium: 43 mg

Iron: 1.1 mg

Fiber: 1.7 g

Sodium: 192 mg

Cholesterol: 14 mg

■ In bowl, mix together all-purpose flour, cornmeal, rolled oats, brown sugar, whole wheat flour, oat bran, bran cereal, baking powder, baking soda, cinnamon and salt.

■ In separate bowl, beat egg; stir in apple, milk and oil. Quickly stir all at once into dry ingredients until just mixed. Spread evenly in lightly greased 8-inch (2 L) square cake pan. Sprinkle with wheat germ.

■ Bake in 350°F (180°C) oven for 40 minutes or until tester inserted in center comes out clean. Makes 16 squares.

## Blueberry Cinnamon Muffins

**Per Muffin:**

Calories: 178

Fat: 5.2 g

Protein: 3.2 g

Carbohydrate: 30.4 g

Calcium: 69 mg

Iron: 1.4 mg

Fiber: 1.6 g

Sodium: 140 mg

Cholesterol: 21 mg

*Frozen blueberries let us enjoy muffins like these all year round. It's worth making sure the blueberries are the small wild variety. For a seasonal touch, replace half of the blueberries with halved cranberries.*

| | | |
|---|---|---|
| 1 cup | all-purpose flour | 250 mL |
| 1/2 cup | whole wheat flour | 125 mL |
| 1 tbsp | cinnamon | 15 mL |
| 2 tsp | baking powder | 10 mL |
| 1/4 tsp | baking soda | 1 mL |
| 3/4 cup | packed brown sugar | 175 mL |
| 1 | egg | 1 |
| 3/4 cup | 2% milk | 175 mL |
| 1/4 cup | margarine or butter, melted | 50 mL |
| 1 tsp | vanilla | 5 mL |
| 1-1/2 cups | blueberries, fresh or thawed | 375 mL |
| 4 tsp | granulated sugar | 20 mL |

■ In large bowl, stir together all-purpose and whole wheat flours, half of the cinnamon, the baking powder and baking soda; blend in brown sugar.

■ In separate bowl, beat egg; mix in milk, margarine or butter and vanilla. Stir into flour mixture along with berries, just until moistened.

■ Spoon into large greased or paper-lined muffin cups, filling to top. Combine granulated sugar with remaining cinnamon; sprinkle over muffins. Bake in 375°F (190°C) oven for about 25 minutes or until firm to the touch. Makes 11 muffins.

*Blueberry Cinnamon Muffins*

## Crunchy Banana Bread

**Per Slice:**

Calories: 175

Fat: 2.5 g

Protein: 4.5 g

Carbohydrate: 35 g

Calcium: 45 mg

Iron: 1.7 mg

Fiber: 1.8 g

Sodium: 190 mg

Cholesterol: 37 mg

*This bread gets its unique texture from millet. Substitute 1/2 cup (125 mL) buttermilk for the milk and vinegar, if desired.*

| | | |
|---|---|---|
| 1/2 cup | 2% milk | 125 mL |
| 1-1/2 tsp | white vinegar | 7 mL |
| 1 cup | graham flour | 250 mL |
| 1 cup | all-purpose flour | 250 mL |
| 1 tsp | baking powder | 5 mL |
| 1 tsp | baking soda | 5 mL |
| 1/4 tsp | salt | 1 mL |
| 3/4 cup | packed brown sugar | 175 mL |
| 1 tbsp | margarine or butter, softened | 15 mL |
| 1 cup | mashed bananas | 250 mL |
| 2 | eggs, beaten | 2 |
| 1/3 cup | millet | 75 mL |

■ Combine milk and vinegar; set aside. Mix together graham and all-purpose flours, baking powder, baking soda and salt; set aside.

■ In bowl, blend sugar with margarine or butter. Add bananas and eggs, beating well. Stir in flour mixture alternately with sour milk, beating well after each addition. Stir in millet.

■ Pour into waxed-paper-lined 9- × 5-inch (2 L) loaf pan. Bake in 350°F (180°C) oven for 45 to 50 minutes or until browned and tester inserted in center comes out clean. Let cool in pan for 5 minutes. Turn out onto rack and let cool completely. Makes 12 slices.

## Whole Wheat Pretzels

*Homemade pretzels are best served fresh from the oven, but you can also cool them and store them in the freezer for handy snacks anytime. Packed into lunch bags in the morning, they'll be thawed and ready to eat by lunchtime. If you're making these for children, you may want to reduce the amount of pepper.*

| | | |
|---|---|---|
| 1 | pkg active dry yeast (or 1 tbsp/15 mL) | 1 |
| 1-1/2 tsp | granulated sugar | 7 mL |
| 1-1/2 cups | warm water | 375 mL |
| 2 tbsp | vegetable oil | 25 mL |
| 1-3/4 cups | whole wheat flour | 425 mL |
| 1-3/4 cups | (approx) all-purpose flour | 425 mL |
| 1 tsp | salt | 5 mL |
| 1/4 cup | sesame seeds | 50 mL |
| 1 tsp | freshly ground pepper | 5 mL |
| 1 | egg, beaten | 1 |

**Per Pretzel:**

Calories: 69

Fat: 2 g

Protein: 2.3 g

Carbohydrate: 10.9 g

Calcium: 7 mg

Iron: 0.7 mg

Fiber: 1 g

Sodium: 79 mg

Cholesterol: 7 mg

■ In large bowl, combine yeast and sugar; pour in water and let stand for 5 minutes or until frothy. Stir in oil.

■ Stir whole wheat flour, 1 cup (250 mL) of the all-purpose flour and salt into yeast mixture; gradually add enough of the remaining all-purpose flour to make smooth but sticky dough.

■ Turn out dough onto lightly floured surface; knead in half of the sesame seeds and all the pepper. Knead dough for 10 minutes or until smooth and elastic.

■ Cut dough into 30 pieces. Roll each piece into rope about 8 inches (20 cm) long and 1/2 inch (1 cm) in diameter. Curve each rope into a U-shape. Twist ends around each other; place twisted end on loop of dough, pinching lightly to seal. Place pretzels on lightly greased baking sheet. Brush with beaten egg and sprinkle with remaining sesame seeds.

■ Bake in 400°F (200°C) oven for 20 to 25 minutes or until puffed and golden. Let cool and store in airtight containers in freezer. Makes 30 pretzels.

## Apricot Snacking Cake

**Per Serving:**

Calories: 114

Fat: 3.8 g

Protein: 2.6 g

Carbohydrate: 18.9 g

Calcium: 32 mg

Iron: 1.3 mg

Fiber: 2 g

Sodium: 99 mg

Cholesterol: 0 mg

*Not only is this eggless cake high in dietary fiber, it's also cholesterol-free.*

| | | |
|---|---|---|
| 1 cup | whole wheat flour | 250 mL |
| 2/3 cup | wheat germ | 150 mL |
| 1/2 cup | all-purpose flour | 125 mL |
| 1/2 cup | packed brown sugar | 125 mL |
| 2-1/2 tsp | baking powder | 12 mL |
| 1 tsp | cinnamon | 5 mL |
| 1/2 tsp | salt | 2 mL |
| 3/4 cup | orange juice | 175 mL |
| 1/4 cup | vegetable oil | 50 mL |
| 1 cup | snipped dried apricots (about 20) | 250 mL |

**Nutty Topping:**

| | | |
|---|---|---|
| 2 tbsp | finely chopped nuts | 25 mL |
| 1 tbsp | wheat germ | 15 mL |
| 1 tbsp | brown sugar | 15 mL |

■ In bowl, combine whole wheat flour, wheat germ, all-purpose flour, sugar, baking powder, cinnamon and salt. Whisk together orange juice and oil; quickly stir into dry ingredients just until moistened. Fold in apricots. Spread in greased 9-inch (2.5 L) square cake pan.

**Nutty Topping:** Combine nuts, wheat germ and sugar; sprinkle over batter, gently pressing into place.

■ Bake in 350°F (180°C) oven for 25 minutes or until golden brown and cake tester inserted in center comes out clean. Let cool in pan. Makes 20 pieces.

**AN APPLE A DAY. . .**
**Fruits and fruit juices make low-calorie, vitamin-rich snacks any time of the day. Bite into a seasonal fruit during the summer — or enjoy apples, bananas, pears, or dried fruits year-round.**

## Crunchy Seed Cookies

*Really more like an English biscuit than what we call a cookie, these treats, which provide more fiber than most cookies, go well with cheese.*

| | | |
|---|---|---|
| 1/2 cup | all-purpose flour | 125 mL |
| 1/2 cup | whole wheat flour | 125 mL |
| 1/2 cup | wheat germ | 125 mL |
| 1/4 cup | oat bran | 50 mL |
| 1 tsp | cinnamon | 5 mL |
| 1/2 tsp | salt | 2 mL |
| 1/3 cup | margarine or butter | 75 mL |
| 1/2 cup | packed brown sugar | 125 mL |
| 1 | egg | 1 |
| 1 tsp | vanilla | 5 mL |
| 2 tbsp | each sunflower, sesame and poppy seeds | 25 mL |

**Per Cookie:**

Calories: 42

Fat: 2.1 g

Protein: 1.1 g

Carbohydrate: 4.9 g

Calcium: 12 mg

Iron: 0.4 mg

Fiber: 0.5 g

Sodium: 43 mg

Cholesterol: 4 mg

■ Mix together all-purpose and whole wheat flours, wheat germ, oat bran, cinnamon and salt.

■ In bowl, cream margarine or butter and brown sugar until light; beat in egg and vanilla. Stir in dry ingredients; mix well. Stir in sunflower, sesame and poppy seeds.

■ Between 2 sheets of waxed paper, roll out dough, in batches, to 1/8-inch (3 mm) thickness. With cookie cutter, cut into 2-1/2-inch (6 cm) rounds. Bake on ungreased baking sheets in 350°F (180°C) oven for 8 to 10 minutes or until lightly browned. Let cool for 5 minutes on baking sheets. Makes 4 dozen cookies.

# Healthy Eating and You

## Guidelines for Healthy Eating

As we mentioned in the Introduction to this cookbook, eating light isn't just a matter of cutting back on fat or calories. It's also a matter of eating right. And that means choosing a variety of foods every day that are rich in nutrients and low in fat — and eating them in moderation to maintain a healthy weight.

### Eat a Variety of Foods Each Day

Choose a wide variety of foods to ensure that you get all the nutrients you need, in sufficient amounts for good health. By eating different foods every day, you also avoid getting too much of any one food, especially high-fat foods.

Plan your meals throughout the day so that you include the following foods:
- Legumes: beans, lentils, split peas
- Grain foods: breads, cereals, rice, pasta
- Fruits and vegetables
- Lower-fat milk, yogurt and cheese
- Leaner cuts of meat, poultry and fish.

### Cut Back on Dietary Fat

North Americans eat too much fat, a factor that is linked with several serious health problems including heart disease, certain cancers, gastrointestinal problems and being overweight. To eat less dietary fat:
- Use less total fat: butter, margarine, shortening, cooking oil, salad dressings and mayonnaise.
- Use lower-fat (2% or less butter fat) milk, yogurt and cottage cheese; replace regular cheeses with lower-fat cheeses (15% or less butter fat) most of the time; use lower-fat sherbet, frozen yogurt and frozen desserts instead of ice cream.
- Serve smaller portions of the leanest cuts of meat.
- Cook foods using as little added fat as possible (and use a nonstick pan).
- Limit the amount of fast food, snack foods and desserts you eat.

### Eat More Complex Carbohydrate (Starchy) Foods

Healthy eaters are changing their eating habits so that more of the calories they consume in a day come from starchy or complex carbohydrates rather than from fat. It's quite easy to make this change:
- Start your day with cereal for breakfast.
- Choose a lentil soup and a whole wheat roll for lunch.
- Base your evening meal on starchy foods like rice or pasta with lots of vegetables — and use higher-fat, protein-rich foods like meat, eggs and cheese in smaller amounts to round out the meal.

The following foods are high in complex carbohydrates:
- All grain-based foods: breads, cereals, pasta, rice and barley
- Foods made with flour
- Legumes: beans, lentils, split peas
- All vegetables, especially potatoes, corn, lima beans, peas, turnips and yams.

### Eat More Dietary Fiber

North Americans are being advised to increase their intake of dietary fiber. Higher-fiber diets are known to regulate the bowel and are linked with a reduced risk for heart disease, certain cancers and better blood sugar management for those with diabetes. Often, you will get complex carbohydrates and fiber together if you choose the whole grain form of a starchy food like bread or rice.

The following foods are high in dietary fiber:
- Foods made from whole grains: oatmeal, whole wheat, corn meal, brown rice
- Brans: corn, oat, rice and wheat
- Legume-based meals: baked beans, lentil casseroles, split pea soup, bean salads
- Fruits and vegetables
- Dried fruits
- Nuts and seeds.

## Limit Salt, Alcohol and Caffeine

For general good health, limit the amount of salt you add to foods either in cooking or at the table. Packaged convenience foods, fast foods and most snack foods are high in salt — enjoy them in moderation.

Alcohol use should be kept to a moderate intake, considered to be no more than 1 or 2 drinks in a day. A drink is: 5 oz/150 mL wine; 1 bottle of beer; 1-1/2 oz/45 mL spirits.

North Americans get most of their caffeine from coffee and tea drinking. A moderate intake of caffeine — 400 to 450 mg of caffeine, an amount found in 3 to 4 cups of coffee daily — is considered harmless.

## Remember Calcium: It's Important!

A lot of people today, especially women, are staying away from milk and other dairy products because of the saturated fats these foods contain.

By not drinking milk, you may be cutting back a little on fat but you're also cutting back a lot on calcium — and calcium is a mineral of critical importance in the development and maintenance of bone health. Milk products, including low-fat and skim milk, are still the best source of dietary calcium and are also rich in other important nutrients such as protein and riboflavin. You can also get calcium from whole grain foods, legumes and dark green vegetables.

# Understanding the Nutrient Chart with Each Recipe

Every recipe in this cookbook is analyzed for a selection of nutrients. To compare the nutrient contribution of a recipe to your overall nutrient needs in a day, we have designed this easy reference chart.

### *Canadian Living*'s Selected Nutrient Guide for Ages 25-49

|  | Woman | Man |
|---|---|---|
| Calories (Energy) | 1900 | 2700 |
| Fat (grams) | 63 | 90 |
| Protein (grams) | 51 | 64 |
| Carbohydrate (grams) | 260 | 370 |
| Calcium (milligrams) | 700 | 800 |
| Iron (milligrams) | 13 | 9 |
| Fiber (grams) | 25-35 | 25-35 |
| Sodium (milligrams) | 3000 or less | 3000 or less |
| Cholesterol (milligrams) | 300 | 300 |

The values above are based on several sources of information:
*Recommended Nutrient Intakes, 1990*; Canada's *Nutrition Recommendations*; the scientific literature.
The values for carbohydrate and fat have been calculated from advice given in *Nutrition Recommendations*.
At this time, there are no Canadian quantitative statements about fiber and sodium intakes. However, there are intake levels of both fiber and sodium which are generally recognized as being consistent with good health. These values are listed above to give general guidance.

## How to Use This Chart

The values in this chart are target nutrient intakes for the average person aged 25-49 with a moderate activity level. They are not values that are carved in stone. Treat them as a general nutrient guide, keeping in mind that on some days, you may get more of some nutrients; on other days, less.

More active individuals may need more calories and more of those nutrients closely tied with calorie intake, namely carbohydrate and fat. Likewise, more sedentary people may need fewer calories, carbohydrate and fat.

## What About Adults of Different Ages?

The values given here can be used for adults of other ages as well. Although there are small differences in the needs for some nutrients, the differences are minor — with the exception of calories, carbohydrate and fat. Generally, younger adults will need more calories and, therefore, can afford a few more grams of both carbohydrate and fat in their daily diet. Older adults, especially older men, will require fewer calories and should, therefore, aim for a lower carbohydrate and fat intake.

# The Contributors

**Margaret Fraser** contributes regularly to *Canadian Living* and is a former associate food editor of the magazine. She is also the editor of *Canadian Living*'s Microwave, Barbecue and Rush-Hour cookbooks and is currently researching a book on Canadian cooking through the decades of the 20th century. Her weekly column on microwave cooking appears in *The Toronto Sun*.

**Elizabeth Baird** is food director of *Canadian Living* magazine. She is also the author of several bestselling cookbooks and is a leading name on the Canadian culinary scene. She is currently at work on *Country Cooking*, the next cookbook in the *Canadian Living* series, which will be published in the fall of 1991.

**Bonnie Baker Cowan** is editor of *Canadian Living* and has been a frequent contributor to the magazine's food pages, both as writer and as editor.

**Nancy Enright** is a food writer and the author of *Nancy Enright's Canadian Herb Cookbook*.

**Carol Ferguson** is one of Canada's best-known food writers and is also the editor of *The Canadian Living Entertaining Cookbook* and *The Canadian Living Cookbook*.

**Patricia Jamieson** was manager of *Canadian Living*'s Test Kitchen for 4 years until her move last year to *Eating Well* magazine, a publication of Telemedia (U.S.) in Vermont.

**Anne Lindsay** is a food writer, consultant and author of the bestselling cookbooks, *Smart Cooking* and *The Lighthearted Cookbook*. A new cookbook, *Lighthearted Everyday Cooking*, will be published in the spring of 1991.

**Beth C. Moffatt** is a freelance home economist, food stylist and food writer.

**Gordon Morash** is a food writer with *The Edmonton Journal* and also does radio commentaries on food for the CBC.

**Rose Murray** is a freelance food writer, consultant, broadcaster and author of several cookbooks. Her most recent cookbook is *Canadian Christmas Cooking*.

**Iris Raven** is a freelance food writer for *Canadian Living* and also works frequently in the Test Kitchen.

**Kay Spicer** is a home economist, food consultant and journalist. Her most recent cookbook is *From Mom With Love—Real Home Cooking*. She is also the author of *Light & Easy Choices* and *Light & Easy Choice Desserts*.

**Bonnie Stern** is proprietor of The Bonnie Stern School of Cooking in Toronto. She is also a food writer, broadcaster, columnist and the author of several popular cookbooks, most recently *Appetizers by Bonnie Stern*.

**Lucy Waverman** is director of The Cooking School in Toronto and is also a food writer, consultant, teacher and author of several cookbooks.

*Canadian Living*'s **Test Kitchen** developed many new recipes for this book and also created lighter versions of popular recipes from the magazine.

# Photography Credits

**Craig Aurness/First Light:** front and back covers (background); title page (background).

**Fred Bird:** front cover (food); back cover (food/right); title page (food/top and bottom right); pages 9, 10, 12, 15, 19, 20, 23, 26, 31, 32, 34, 37, 39, 43, 44, 56, 59, 61, 62, 66, 69, 73, 74, 91, 103, 104, 107, 108, 112, 115, 116, 120, 125, 126, 128, 131, 133.

**Christopher Campbell:** pages 85, 123.

**Clive Champion:** page 65.

**Nino D'Angelo:** page 52.

**Ron Elmy:** page 119.

**Frank Grant:** page 86.

**Michael Kohn:** page 48.

**Gary Rhijnburger:** page 96.

**John Stephens:** pages 29, 51, 54, 99.

**Clive Webster:** pages 24, 83.

**Robert Wigington:** back cover (food/left); pages 70, 100, 111.

**Stanley Wong:** title page (food/bottom left); pages 17, 41, 47, 77, 80, 94.

# Special Thanks

The publisher would like to thank Iris Raven for her energy and hard work in the Test Kitchen during the creation and revising of recipes for this book. Special thanks to Sharyn Joliat and Barbara Selley of Info Access for the many long hours they spent compiling and organizing the nutrient data for each recipe, to Denise Beatty for her invaluable advice, and to Elizabeth Baird for her suggestions and her help in structuring this book.

# Index and Recipe Credits

Design and Art Direction:   Gordon Sibley Design Inc.

Editorial Director:   Hugh Brewster

Project Editor:   Wanda Nowakowska

Editorial Assistance:   Beverley Renahan
Catherine Fraccaro

Nutrient Analysis:   Info Access

Nutrition Consultant:   Denise Beatty

Production Director:   Susan Barrable

Production Assistance:   Donna Chong

Typography:   On-line Graphics

Color Separation:   Colour Technologies

Printing and Binding:   Friesen Printers

Canadian Living Advisory Board:   Robert A. Murray
Bonnie Baker Cowan
Elizabeth Baird
Anna Hobbs

*The Canadian Living Light and Healthy Cookbook*
*was produced by Madison Press Books*
*under the direction of Albert E. Cummings.*